THE LIFE AND DEATH OF RICHARD III

Anthony Cheetham CBE was born in Mexico City and educated at Eton and Balliol College, Oxford, where he read Modern History. Over the course of a sixty-year career in book publishing, he has established many of the UK's most prominent publishing companies including Century, Orion, Quercus and Head of Zeus.

He lives in London and Gloucestershire.

ANTHONY CHEETHAM

THE LIFE AND DEATH OF RICHARD III

INTRODUCTION BY DAN JONES

HEAD of ZEUS

First published in the UK in 1972 by Weidenfeld and Nicolson Ltd
and Book Club Associates
Reissued in the UK in 2025 by Head of Zeus Ltd
This paperback edition published in the UK in 2026 by Head of Zeus Ltd

9 7 5 3 1 2 4 6 8

A catalogue record for this book is available from the British Library.

ISBN (PB): 9781035915187
ISBN (E): 9781035915163

Typeset by Six Red Marbles India
Printed and Bound in Great Britain
by Clays Ltd, Elcograf S.p.A.

MIX
Paper | Supporting responsible forestry
FSC® C018072

Bloomsbury Publishing Plc
50 Bedford Square, London, WC1B 3DP, UK
Bloomsbury Publishing Ireland Limited
29 Earlsfort Terrace, Dublin 2, D02 AY28, Ireland

HEAD OF ZEUS LTD
5–8 Hardwick Street
London EC1R 4RG

To find out more about our authors and books
visit www.headofzeus.com
For product safety related questions contact productsafety@bloomsbury.com

Contents

Foreword

The most controversial king in English history – his passionate admirers would still not deny this title to Richard III, while continuing to see in him the most maligned of our sovereigns. As for those nourished beyond redemption on the black legend of Crookback Dick, even they must admit that his reign contains a spectacular historical problem in the deaths of the princes in the tower, the exact truth about which is still not known even after a lapse of over five hundred years. Of course the trouble with this type of riddle, as Anthony Cheetham ably shows in a highly readable new biography, is that, although it arouses the detective instinct in us all, at the same time there is the risk of its overshadowing the whole reign – to say nothing of the true personality of the man himself.

Thus it is especially valuable to have the fact of Richard's early life unrolled, including his own position in the complex family tree of York and Lancaster, for without this it is impossible to assess the man. It is a youth of promise, both military and administrative, including a decisive action at Tewkesbury and excellent handling of the North on his brother's behalf, as a result of which he was termed by those in a position to know 'our full tender especial good lord of York'. By the age of thirty he had been made Hereditary Warden of the Western Marches of Scotland by Edward as a reward for his good services to the Crown. Hard-working, brave, small in stature but still handsome (not in fact a hunchback, although one shoulder may have been slightly higher than the other), the ascetic figure of Richard presents a strong contrast to his brother the king, a golden-haired giant in youth but becoming 'overweight and oversexed' with age, and loaded with the problems that his indulgent marriage to Elizabeth Woodville had landed on the country in the shape of her grasping relations.

Indeed it is in this contrast that Anthony Cheetham looks for the source of Richard's trouble with the old régime on his brother's death; this plodding, even Puritanical, character, disliking the free and easy ways of his brother's Court. Even the usurpation is seen in the context of the terrible disaster that the minority of a child king could bring upon a country, Richard in his short reign concentrating on much constructive work towards better government. There still remains the problem of the young princes' fate: here Anthony Cheetham is in no sense concerned to whitewash his subject. He contributes instead a lucid discussion of the evidence – showing incidentally how much of it derives from subsequent Tudor propaganda – at the end of which he demonstrates how, if Richard was guilty, at least it accords with the straightforward personality of the man, a man who was so far from being Shakespeare's calculating villain that he probably possessed if anything 'too little guile rather than too much'.

Introduction

In the bleak dark of the early morning on Monday 22 August 1485, King Richard III of England rose from a fitful sleep. Lying in camp with his army he had been tormented by visions of 'evil spirits haunting evidently about him [which] would not let him rest'. Richard had awoken with an empty belly and a guilty conscience. But the hour was so small that there was no breakfast to be found, and no priest awake to absolve him. Thus began, inauspiciously, the last day of his life.

A few hours later Richard III – usurper and regicide – led his men into battle in a desperate attempt to cling to his crown. In this he was no different from most other English kings of his century: the fifteenth century, a time when Fortune's Wheel span as fast as a fairground ride. Henry IV, Henry VI and Edward IV had all enjoyed uncertain claims to royal office and all had found themselves at war, with life and throne at stake. Henry Tudor – the man who now challenged Richard at Bosworth Field – would have to walk through the fire in his turn.

Becoming a king in this age was more often a matter of self-help than simple inheritance. Remaining king could be a white-knuckle ride. 'Within the hollow crown,' wrote Shakespeare, much later, 'that rounds the mortal temples of a king, keeps death his court.' Death found Richard at Bosworth that day. He was hacked down in the thick of battle, stripped naked, mutilated and thrown in a shallow grave. His fate was not merely to be the last of the Plantagenet kings who had ruled England for more than three hundred years. He was also doomed to be remembered as a villain.

In popular imagination and English dramatic tradition, Richard has come, over the centuries since his death, to embody in one crooked person all the evils of his time. Shakespeare's portrait – of a hunchbacked spider, spinning a dark web in which he will become fatally entangled – is so memorable and perfectly written that it has become a staple of the theatrical canon: a role against which every serious actor since Richard Burbage has had to test himself.

Like all Shakespeare's best historical characters, the Richard who lopes onto stage declaring an end to the winter of his discontent is both an outrageous libel and a stinging version of the truth. Shakespeare more often proceeds by distortion than pure invention and so it is with his Richard. The cleverness, ruthlessness, calculated self-interest and physical debility are all drawn from life, but in monstrous ratio. Richard's more appealing qualities – concern for the plight of the poor; heroic endurance in the face of disability and childhood trauma – are passed over with barely a flick of the pen. Still, like the caricature of a London street artist or newspaper cartoonist, all that is there is real: wickedly rearranged but somehow capturing a spirit of the truth.

Newspaper cartoons and dramatic libels, however, will not do for historians. So it is that Richard, whose reign lasted just two years and two months but comprise ceaseless sequence of hair-raising incident, has be the subject of many biographies during the last hal millennium. Thomas More wrote the first substantial lif around 1513. The most recent full-length scholarly study, by Professor Michael Hicks, appeared in 2021. Between and around these have appeared countless other portraits, ranging in tone from scandalised denunciation to one-eyed apologia.

Inevitably, studies of Richard have often been works in conversation with their times. More's critical biography was written within living memory of Richard's death, during the early reign of Henry VIII, when it was hoped that the 'cruelty, mischief, and trouble of the tempestuous world' that was England in the 1480s could now be safely put to bed.

During the seventeenth century, the writer Thomas Wincoll turned to Richard's reign as a political allegory for the horrors of the English Civil War, in a narrative poem whose title made clear where the author's feelings lay: Wincoll's work was entitled *Plantagenets Tragicall Story: Or, The Death of King Edward the Fourth: With The unnaturall Voyage of Richard the Third through the Red Sea of his Nephews innocent blood, to his usurped Crowne*. In our own times, as historical sentiment has drifted towards a vogue for victimhood and underdog narrative, studies have been published under such titles as *Richard III: The Maligned King*.

Whenever their age and whatever their inclinations, however, each of Richard's biographers has had to wrestle with the same dark matter. How and why did Richard, Duke of Gloucester, the Yorkist stalwart, whose motto was 'loyaulte me lie' [loyalty binds me] become the man who burned the house down? To what extent was he the victim of interesting times, and to what extent the architect? Who was he? And what, deep down, did he want?

Richard being Richard, this is not straightforward. Since the second half of the twentieth century, the last of the Plantagenets has not only been the property of theatre directors and historians. He has also become the subject of a cottage industry and campaigning movement focused on what amounts to a form of judicial review. Ricardianism is the catch-all term, and it is as much a doctrinal sect as a medieval subdiscipline.

Ricardians can be academics or amateurs, but all are

by definition enthusiasts. Their concerns are with matters historical: why did the stalwart loyalist Richard decide in 1483 to seize the throne from his brother Edward IV's eldest son, the uncrowned Edward V? Was it true (as virtually everyone at the time believed, and as political common sense would surely have dictated) that Richard ordered the murders of that boy and his brother, better known as the Princes in the Tower? If not, at whom should we point our accusing fingers? The problem with Ricardianism is that it very often proceeds from a foregone conclusion, at every turn striving to present us with a king who either did no wrong, or was at any rate the best of a bad bunch.

Anthony Cheetham's life of Richard III was first published in 1972, as part of a series of monarchical biographies edited by Antonia Fraser. More than half a century since it first appeared, it remains a fine, crisply written and judicious biography, which presents Richard's life in the round. It is by no means a piece of uncritical Ricardiana, but Cheetham's treatment of 'Old Dick' is generous and humane. His Richard is no criminal mastermind, but a limited strategist: a draughts player trying his hand for the first time at chess.

Cheetham takes his time to show us Richard before the fall: a 'soldier and administrator with a distaste for courtly intrigues and political infighting'. When the catastrophes of 1483 begin with his brother Edward IV's sudden, glutton's death, Richard's 'reaction to each succeeding crisis bears the mark of an impulsive man of action taking the short cut to his immediate objective without pausing to work out the long-term effects. If Richard is to be judged, then he must be accused not of too much guile, but of too little.'

Cheetham's Richard is not excused his many sins. His claim to the throne, based on the argument that the Princes in the Tower were illegitimate, is 'a legal fiction'. Alternative candidates for the boys' murder are seriously considered, but in the end Richard is arraigned as 'prime suspect'; the deed 'leaves an ineradicable stain on Richard's character'; and it proves 'a colossal blunder'.

All the same, if Richard is unabsolved, he is not entirely villainised. When we leave him at the end of chapter eight, he is dead, but his memory lives on, still dear to the hearts of many who knew him, particularly poor men whose plight Richard's legal reforms aimed to help. Placed next to Henry VII, Richard hardly appears exceptional in his iniquity. Everyone has blood on their hands. Richard is merely the unlucky loser.

When this book was first published, the most recent significant evidential discovery concerning the fate of the Princes in the Tower was the exhumation of two boys' skeletons beneath a staircase in the Tower of London. These were found during the reign of Charles II; the remains lie today in an urn made for them by Sir Christopher Wren.

In the intervening years an even more exciting skeleton

has been turned up. In 2012 archaeologists working on the lost foundations of the church of the Greyfriars in Leicester turned up human remains that were identified as Richard's. The story of that dig and subsequent scientific analysis of the bones became a world news event, which was recounted in an excellent TV documentary and more recently retold in a feature film.

Data emerging from the Leicester study has provided important scholarly insights into Richard's life and his final hours. (It has also encouraged the wildest fantasies of Ricardianism.) No biography of Richard can be considered complete today unless it makes reference to this valuable work. I have therefore added a ninth chapter to this book, summarising events in Leicester and explaining how they affect current scholarly thinking about Richard.

My work, however, is really just an appendix. Anthony Cheetham's biography easily stands the test of the years since its first publication, enjoyable not only for the precision of its judgements but for the lucidity and stylish economy of its prose. Elegant, witty, brisk, pithy and always to the point – these are qualities that characterise not just Anthony Cheetham the writer but Anthony Cheetham the man.

It has been my privilege to be published by Anthony for most of my career, and during that time I have spent many enjoyable and enlightening hours in conversation with him, often perfumed by the sweet smell of his cigarette smoke and a glass of Meursault. I have learned more about publishing from him than anyone else, and have come, like so many others, to treasure his wisdom and the stimulation of his company.

In *The Life and Death of Richard III*, Anthony reminds us that his brilliant instincts as a publisher are founded on his own considerable talents as a historian and writer. I am honoured to have been asked to introduce and expand this new edition of his fine biography, which richly deserves its return to the bookshelves, and I hope that I have done him and his notorious subject justice.

Dan Jones
Staines-upon-Thames
Autumn 2024

1

York and Lancaster

1452–61

At the Northamptonshire castle of Fotheringhay, on 2 October 1452, Cecily, Duchess of York, gave birth to a son, who was christened Richard after his father. The Duchess was renowned for her beauty and for her enduring devotion to her husband. Known as 'the Rose of Raby', she had married comparatively late, in her mid-twenties, and accompanied her husband on his tours of duty in the French territories conquered by Henry V and in the Irish pale. Undaunted by the hazards of war, travel or continual pregnancy, she had already borne ten children in three different countries before the young Richard first saw the light of day. Six of these children – three boys and three girls – had survived the rigours of infancy: in 1452 Richard's eldest brother Edward was ten years old, Edmund was nine and George was four.

All three inherited something of their mother's looks and robust constitution. Richard, the last of Cecily's surviving children, seems to have inherited neither: a weak and sickly child, he struggled through his early years, causing an anonymous rhymster to comment, with a note of surprise, that 'Richard liveth yet'. In looks and height he would later resemble his father, a shortish man with plain, forthright features.

Richard, Duke of York, was the greatest magnate and landowner in the kingdom, excepting the king himself. From his mother, Anne Mortimer, he inherited the vast Welsh border estates of the earldom of March, the earldom of Ulster and the Irish lordships of Connaught,

Trim and Clare; from his father, Richard, Earl of Cambridge, the dukedom of York and the earldoms of Rutland and Cambridge. Through both his parents York also inherited the royal blood of Edward III. On the one side he traced his descent from Lionel, Duke of Clarence, second son of Edward III; on the other he was the grandson of Edward III's fourth son, Edmund of Langley. These family relationships are of more than passing interest: their shadow lies across the short and violent span of Richard's life, and stains the whole chapter of English history known as the Wars of the Roses.

The fortunes of the House of York were founded on the fact that their royal descent was arguably better than that of the reigning House of Lancaster. For, while York could claim descent from the second son of Edward III, Henry VI could trace his only from Edward's third son, John of Gaunt. King Henry thus owed his crown more to the successful usurpation of his grandfather, Henry Bolingbroke, than to the legitimate laws of inheritance.

These dynastic subtleties might well have remained purely academic, if the kingdom had not been wracked, in the years preceding Richard's birth, by a series of crises that left the king bankrupt, the barons at each others' throats and the country shorn of its empire overseas. King Henry himself was most to blame. At a time when the king was expected to be his own prime minister and commander in chief combined, Henry was interested only in charity and prayer. This saintly incompetent allowed his

HENRY
THE SIXTH

ministers to pillage the royal coffers to the tune of about £24,000 a year. Nor was he able to devise an effective policy towards the besetting problem of his dwindling possessions in France. Henry V's great conquests had saddled his son with an embarrassing legacy – crushingly expensive to maintain, humiliating to abandon. In 1444 his advisers persuaded the king that he must cut his losses, come to terms with the French and marry a French princess. The bride chosen by Henry's advisers was Margaret of Anjou, daughter of René, Duke of Anjou, and niece of the French King, Charles VII. Although she was only fifteen years old, Margaret's dazzling looks, her lively intelligence and her impetuous energy soon wrought a transformation in the routine of her husband's Court. With more gratitude than foresight she also linked her fortunes – and the king's – with the second-rate ministers who had made her a Queen. But the French truce negotiated by her favourite protégé, William de la Pole, Earl (later Marquess and Duke) of Suffolk, lasted only two years. In 1448 the province of Maine was ceded to the French: in 1449 Normandy went the same way. By now the country was baying for the blood of the appeasers whom it held responsible for these disasters – Suffolk, Somerset and Queen Margaret.

In the following spring discontent boiled over into open rebellion. Suffolk was assassinated. Jack Cade and

Henry VI, a portrait by an unknown artist.

an army of Kentish rebels marched on London and forced the king to flee from his own capital. The Bishop of Salisbury was murdered by his flock who 'spoiled him unto the naked skin, and rent his bloody shirt into pieces and bare them away with them and made boast of their wickedness'.

Someone had to call a halt. Richard, Duke of York had already identified himself as an opponent of the Court party and as a long-standing enemy of John Beaufort, Duke of Somerset. In 1445 Somerset had blocked the renewal of York's appointment as the king's Lieutenant in France. Four years later he had engineered York's removal from the Court to an honourable exile as Lieutenant of Ireland. By 1451 it was also beginning to look as if York, or his eldest son Edward, would one day inherit the Crown. Henry's three uncles had all died childless, and the king still had no children by his French wife.

Cade's rebellion provided York with an excuse to return from Ireland and seek a confrontation with the king. Faced with the evidence of his misgovernment, Henry caved in and agreed to put matters right by consulting his Parliament in October. Parliament was solidly for York. Among the many reforms they demanded were Somerset's imprisonment and York's recognition as the king's chief councillor. But by December Queen Margaret was once again calling the tune. Somerset was reinstated and Parliament was prorogued. When it reassembled in May 1451 one Thomas Young of Bristol was committed

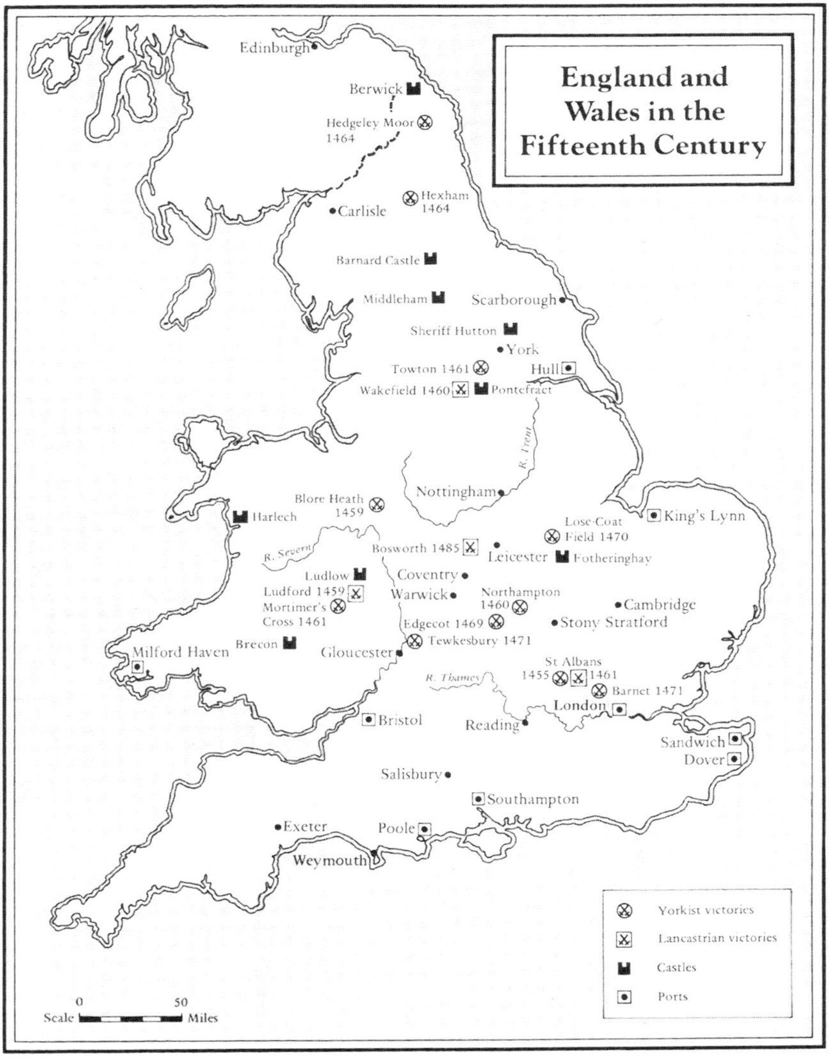
England and Wales in the Fifteenth Century
Edinburgh
Berwick
Hedgeley Moor 1464
Hexham 1464
Carlisle
Barnard Castle
Middleham
Scarborough
Sheriff Hutton
York
Towton 1461
Hull
Wakefield 1460
Pontefract
R. Trent
Nottingham
Blore Heath 1459
Harlech
Lose-Coat Field 1470
King's Lynn
R. Severn
Bosworth 1485
Leicester
Fotheringhay
Ludlow
Coventry
Ludford 1459
Warwick
Northampton 1460
Mortimer's Cross 1461
Cambridge
Edgecot 1469
Stony Stratford
Tewkesbury 1471
Brecon
Milford Haven
Gloucester
St Albans 1455 1461
R. Thames
Barnet 1471
London
Bristol
Reading
Sandwich
Dover
Salisbury
Southampton
Exeter
Poole
Weymouth
Yorkist victories
Lancastrian victories
Castles
Ports
0 50
Scale Miles

The Fifteenth-Century Wool Trade

Wool has been described as 'the flower and strength and revenue and blood of England', and during the late medieval period it was undoubtedly the principal source of wealth to the country. The revenue derived from the trade brought wealth both to secular merchants and to the great monasteries. Thus many of the fine houses and churches built in the fifteenth century were based upon wool.

ABOVE: Dyers at work, from *Des Proprietez des Choses*, a manuscript written in Bruges for Edward IV in 1482, by Jean du Ries.

OPPOSITE: Illustration from Jean de Wavrin's *Chronique d'Angleterre*, the Master of the Staple is shown in audience with Duke Albert of Bavaria.

to the Tower for proposing that York should be named as heir apparent. As far removed from power as ever he was in Ireland, York retired to his castle of Ludlow in the Welsh Marches.

The struggle between the reformers and the Court party had now assumed the character of a vicious personal duel between York and Somerset. With Henry refusing to name his heir, York was afraid that his rival might persuade the Queen to override his legitimate claims. For Somerset too had a claim to the throne through his descent from John of Gaunt and his mistress Catherine Swynford. Early in 1452 York was ready to try again – this time with an army at his back. In a proclamation issued at Ludlow on 3 February, he protested that he was 'the king's true liege man': his reforms had been negated 'through the envy, malice and untruth of the said Duke of Somerset' who 'laboureth continually about the king's Highness for my undoing and to corrupt my blood, and to disherit me and my heirs'. When York's army reached London he found the city's gates closed, and Henry at Blackheath with a force that outnumbered his own. Anxious to avoid bloodshed at any price, the king induced York to surrender on the promise that Somerset would be arrested and tried. But the Queen would not give up the new favourite who had taken Suffolk's place in her affections. The king, always putty in her hands, was induced to break his word. York, who had obediently given himself up, was forced to undergo the humiliation of swearing a public oath never again to take up arms against the king.

Thus, in the year of Richard's birth, the kingdom already teetered on the brink of civil war. In the twelve months that followed, two events of cardinal importance sufficed to push it over the edge. On 17 July 1453 John Talbot, veteran of countless battles and sieges in the English reconquest of France, was killed at the Battle of Castillon, and the last English army in France was annihilated by French cannon. By the year's end Bordeaux had fallen, Guyenne acknowledged Charles VII and the Hundred Years' War was at an end. At Henry's accession thirty years before, the Plantagenet dominions in France had embraced Normandy, Picardy, Ile de France and Gascony: now only Calais and the Channel Islands remained. An irreparable blow was dealt to English pride. Henry's government was branded with the stigma of defeat, and his French Queen became a symbol of England's shame. The defeated soldiers returning from the wars roamed the countryside in armed bands, a menace to the already disintegrating fabric of public order. Most important of all, the loss of empire dissolved the restraining bonds of patriotism that had held the domestic squabbles of the aristocracy in check.

Worse was to follow. Less than a month after Castillon, a bout of insanity deprived King Henry of speech and sense.

Her husband's madness brought out both the best and

the worst in Queen Margaret. Still only twenty-three years old, she devoted her spectacular energy and courage to the defence of Henry's rights. But she was deaf to the real grievances of the Court's political opponents, construing their reforms as a direct assault on the royal prerogatives. While Somerset could do no wrong in her eyes, she had conceived a special loathing for the Duke of York. Without Henry's moderating influence, the Crown now became an instrument of faction. Queen Margaret did not hesitate to press her claims. In October her position was much strengthened when she gave birth to a son, Edward of Lancaster. This was a harsh blow to York's chances but popular feeling still ran high in his favour. The prospect of another long royal minority had little appeal for the Commons who assembled in Parliament early in 1454 to settle the question of the regency. Despite the protests of the Court, Richard of York was declared 'protector and defenser' on 27 March.

The protectorship did not survive the year's end. In December King Henry recovered his wits and formally recognised his son. Somerset, who had been committed to the Tower twelve months previously, was released, and York's ministers were dismissed. Both the Queen and Richard were now set on bringing matters to a head. York withdrew to Sendal Castle in Yorkshire and set about raising an army in conjunction with his brother-in-law, the Earl of Salisbury. The Queen and Somerset summoned their supporters to a meeting of the Great Council at Leicester. The Yorkists mobilised first and marched south, and, with an army of about three thousand men, they collided with the royal army at St Albans. In the first pitched battle of the Wars of the Roses, York was completely victorious. Somerset was slain and the king himself received a flesh wound from a Yorkist arrow.

York's dilemma was that he still claimed to act in the king's name. But, while the king was ruled by the Queen, his only sanction lay in superior force. The next three years were characterised by an armed truce during which the Queen's party slowly regained lost ground. The resurrected protectorship that York forced on the king was again abolished. A hollow reconciliation staged at St Paul's in March 1458 produced no real solutions, and the Duke of York confined himself warily to his estates.

The Yorkists entered the next round of hostilities with only two positive gains. The Merchants of the Staple, the most influential financial organisation in the country, backed them rather than the king as the best hope for a return to good government. The second was that the captaincy of Calais passed, on Somerset's death, to Cecily Neville's young nephew, Richard Neville, Earl of Warwick. Both as a refuge and as a springboard for invasion, Calais was an asset of incalculable value.

As usual the country at large suffered greater hardship than the principals who had brought about the breakdown of central government. The following summary by an anonymous chronicler, though biased in favour of the Yorkists, probably gives a fair picture:

> In this same time, the realm of England was out of all good governance, as it had been many days before, for the king was simple and led by covetous counsel, and owed more than he was worth. His debts increased daily, but payment was there none: all the possessions and lordships that pertained to the crown the king had given away, some to lords and some to other simple persons, so that he had almost nought to live on. And such impositions as were put to the people, as taxes, tallages, and quinzimes, all that came from them was spended on vain, for he held no household he maintained no wars. For these misgovernances, and for many others, the hearts of the people were turned away from them that had the land in governance, and their blessing was turned into cursing.

In Devonshire the Courtenay family terrorised the countryside in pursuit of private vendettas. In Northumberland the Nevilles took full advantage of their temporary ascendancy over the Percies. In 1457 the French launched a raid on Sandwich and burned it to the ground.

Early in 1459, York's youngest son, Richard, then in his seventh year, first felt the impact of war. With the Queen's party openly preparing for an armed challenge, Richard's father no longer considered Fotheringhay a safe refuge for his two younger sons, George and Richard. He therefore decided to move them to the greater isolation and superior defences of his great castle at Ludlow, where they joined his two older boys, the seventeen-year-old Edward, Earl of March, and his sixteen-year-old brother Edmund, Earl of Rutland. As it turned out, this was a most unfortunate decision. By early autumn the Queen's army was gathered at Coventry, poised to march on Ludlow. Despite the arrival of Richard Neville, Earl of Salisbury and his son Warwick, the Duke of York was heavily outnumbered. On the night of 13 October, with the royal army encamped only a mile from Ludlow, he heard that Warwick's most experienced troops – a contingent of the Calais garrison – had defected to seek the king's pardon. The news broke his nerve. The Yorkist leaders took to their heels and made for the Welsh coast. The Duke, who took with him only his elder sons, left his army, his wife and the rest of his family to fend for themselves. He and Edmund sailed for Ireland: Warwick and the others took refuge in Calais.

The Duchess Cecily and her two younger sons were not harshly treated. They were put into the custody of Richard's aunt, the Duchess of Buckingham, and lived on one of Buckingham's manors. In the following year the two boys were attached to the household of Thomas Bourchier, the Archbishop of Canterbury. Late in June 1460 they heard the welcome news that their brother Edward had landed at Sandwich with Salisbury and

Warwick. On 2 July the three earls were welcomed in London, where only the Tower held out for King Henry. Then the Yorkists marched north: once again the Lancastrians were inadequately prepared. When the two armies clashed on 10 July, south of Northampton, the Yorkists carried the day in less than an hour. The Queen had wisely remained in Coventry during the battle and fled with Prince Edward, first to Harlech Castle in Wales, then to Scotland. King Henry was taken in his tent. For a second time he suffered the indignity of being rescued from his councillors in a pitched battle, and was taken back to London to sanction a Yorkist government.

But York, returning from Ireland in mid-September, had more ambitious plans. The clumsy fiction of the protectorship could be taken away as easily as it was granted. On 10 October he informed the astonished Lords in the Painted Chamber that he claimed the Crown by right of inheritance. Many of those present looked on York as a reformer rather than a candidate for the throne, and were not ready to depose the king in his favour. After much debate a compromise was reached: Henry would continue to rule for his natural life, but on his death the Crown would pass to York and his heirs. In the meantime York was to be Prince of Wales, Duke of Cornwall, Earl of Chester – and Protector of the Realm.

While the embarrassed Yorkist lords were arguing over their leader's claims, Queen Margaret was busy canvassing support to put another army in the field. In great secrecy a Lancastrian army was assembled at Hull. She was rewarded with total success. On 9 December York divided his strength, sending Edward west to pacify Wales, while he marched north to deal with the Queen. On the last day of December, the Lancastrians launched a surprise attack on Wakefield where the Protector was lodged. Although heavily outnumbered, York did not run away as he had at Ludlow. He and his son Edmund were killed on the battlefield. His brother-in-law Salisbury was taken and executed. The heads of the Yorkist leaders were impaled on the gates of York. The wars had entered a new and bloodier phase.

For the next three months confusion reigned as the country waited for the final battle that would decide the issue. The Prior of Croyland described the panic engendered by Queen Margaret's northerners as they marched on London:

> ...the northmen... swept onwards like a whirlwind from the north, and in the impulse of their fury attempted to overrun the whole of England. At this period too, fancying that everything tended to insure them freedom from molestation, paupers and beggars flocked forth from those quarters in infinite numbers, just like so many mice rushing forth from their holes, and universally devoted themselves to spoil and rapine, without regard of place or person.... Thus did they proceed with impunity, spreading

> in vast multitudes over a space of thirty miles in breadth, and, covering the whole surface of the earth just like so many locusts, made their way almost to the very walls of London.

Early in February came news that Edward had crushed the earls of Pembroke and Wiltshire at the Battle of Mortimer's Cross. Warwick, who had charge of London, advanced to block the northerners' march on the capital at St Albans. Early in the morning of 17 February the Queen's advance guard entered the town. By mid-afternoon Warwick's left wing had crumbled and he fled westward with the remnants of the army, hoping to join forces with Edward.

London now lay undefended. York's Duchess, who had already lost a husband, a son and a brother, boarded a ship bound for the Low Countries with George and Richard. Mysteriously, Margaret refused to seize the prize that was hers for the taking. Ten days later she had lost her chance. Edward and Warwick entered London in triumph on 26 February. Hugely relieved at their deliverance from the northerners, the citizens gave them a jubilant welcome. But the hero of the hour was Edward of York. Not yet nineteen years old, exceptionally tall and good-looking, he had already given proof of his ability as a commander of men at Mortimer's Cross. After York's death at Wakefield and Warwick's rout at St Albans, only his swift action had saved London from a Lancastrian sacking. He inherited all his father's charms without any of the rancour and suspicion generated by years of political in-fighting. There were no dissenting voices when he was proclaimed King at Paul's Cross on 4 March 1461.

The affair was, of course, carefully staged according to custom with an eye to its propaganda value. The real decision had already been taken by an inner circle of Yorkist leaders meeting at Baynard's Castle. The events leading to Edward's election were described by the City draper Robert Fabyan:

> ...the said earl [of Warwick] caused to be mustered his people in St John's Field, where unto that host were proclaimed and shewed certain articles and points that King Henry had offended in, whereupon it was demanded of the said people whether the said Henry were worthy to reign as king any longer or no. Whereunto the people cried hugely and said, Nay, Nay. And after it was asked of them whether they would have th'earl of March for their king and they cried with one voice, Yea, Yea. After the which admission thus by the commons assented, certain captains were assigned to bear report thereof unto the said earl of March, then being lodged at his

OVERLEAF: The coronation of Edward IV, which took place in Westminster Abbey on 28 June 1461. The King was crowned by Cardinal Bourchier.

> place called Baynard's Castle. Of the which when he was by them ascertained he thanked God and them. And how be it that like a wise prince he shewed by a convenient style that he was insufficient to occupy that great charge for sundry considerations by him then shewed, yet he lastly by the exhortation of the archbishop of Canterbury and the bishop of Exeter and other noble men then present took upon him that charge, and granted to their petition.... Then th'earl of March thus as is abovesaid being elected and admitted for king upon the morrow next ensuing rode unto Paul's and there rode in procession and offered, and there had Te Deum sungen with all solemnity. After which solemnisation finished he was with great royalty conveyed unto Westminster and there in the hall set in the king's see with St Edward's sceptre in his hand.

Edward was, however, careful to postpone his full coronation until he had dealt with Queen Margaret's army, still at large in Yorkshire. He did not want to owe his Crown entirely to the enthusiasm of the Londoners and the backing of the powerful Neville family. The Earl of Warwick, his uncle Lord Fauconberg and John Mowbray, Duke of Norfolk, left the capital first to muster recruits. Edward followed on 13 March. Two weeks later, on Palm Sunday, he led his army onto the field of Towton in a blinding snowstorm. In the longest and bloodiest engagement of the Wars of the Roses the Lancastrian army was completely destroyed. Warwick's brother, George Neville, Bishop of Exeter, reported that the battle 'began with the rising of the sun, and lasted until the tenth hour of the night'. The routed Lancastrians were ruthlessly hunted down and hacked to death until 'so many dead bodies were seen as to cover an area six miles long by three broad and about four furlongs... some 28,000 persons perished on one side and the other'.

'Our puppet', King Henry, accompanied by his wife and son, escaped the slaughter and was granted asylum by the Scots, in exchange for the surrender of the great frontier fortress of Berwick. After resting up for a few days at York, Edward returned to London to claim the Crown, already his by acclamation and by right of conquest.

2

The Kingmaker

1461–71

News of Edward's great victory reached the Duchess of York and her younger sons two weeks later at Utrecht. While the fate of the House of York was in doubt, their welcome had been polite but reserved. Now Duke Philip of Burgundy visited the refugees in person and arranged for a magnificent send-off for them at Bruges. A few days later Richard and George were back in England at the royal manor of Sheen in Surrey.

Since he was only eight years old, it is unlikely that Richard was fully aware of the dizzying changes in his fortunes over the past two and a half years. The débâcle at Ludlow in 1460 left him in the custody of the House of Lancaster, the youngest son of an attainted rebel. A year later his father was Lord Protector and Richard stood fifth in line to the throne. At Wakefield he had lost a father, a brother and an uncle, and had to be smuggled abroad for his safety. Now he was back in England for the crowning of his universally popular brother. An Italian observer recorded that 'words fail me to relate how well the commons love and adore him, as if he were their God. The entire kingdom keeps holiday for the event'.

It was not long before Richard shared in his brother's good fortune. On the eve of Edward's coronation in June Richard and George acted out the elaborate ritual of induction as Knights of the Bath. Four months later, after George had been created Duke of Clarence, Richard in his turn became Duke of Gloucester, and was elected a Knight of the Garter. These titles had little bearing on his immediate future. It was the custom of the time that the sons of the nobility should be boarded out in the household of a family of equivalent rank, where they were known as henchmen. Foreign observers attributed this to the meanness of the English and their lack of affection; and it is probably true that the upper classes in the fifteenth century regarded their children as pawns to their social advancement. There was only one Yorkist lord in the England of 1461 of sufficient rank to take in the king's brother, and that was his cousin Richard Neville, Earl of Warwick.

The pre-eminence of the House of Neville was the supreme example of what inspired matchmaking could do for a family. Warwick's grandfather, Ralph Neville, married Joan Beaufort, bastard daughter of John of Gaunt. His father acquired the earldom of Salisbury through his marriage to the former Earl's daughter, Alice. But the best catch of all was reserved for Warwick himself. He married Anne, the daughter of Richard Beauchamp, Earl of Warwick, owner of a vast inheritance in Wales, the West Country and the Midlands. When the senior branch of the Beauchamps became extinct in 1449 all this, along with the earldom of Warwick, was conferred in his wife's right on the twenty-one-year-old Richard Neville, whose possessions far exceeded those of his father and very nearly equalled those of York himself. The two families – Neville and York – were already closely linked.

Richard, Duke of York had grown up in the household of Warwick's grandfather, Ralph, and had later married Ralph's youngest daughter, Cecily. Marriage thus supplied the sinews of the tripartite alliance of Warwick, Salisbury and York that enabled those two Houses to take on the king and most of the older aristocracy.

Like all great landowners of the time Warwick had no permanent residence: but his favourite castle, and the home of his Countess, was at Middleham, capital of Wensleydale in the North Riding of Yorkshire. The massive keep, built by Robert Fitzralf in the 1170s and acquired by the Nevilles in the thirteenth century, still stands today, along with the gatehouse and the chapel. Here Richard was to spend the better part of the next four years.

He and his fellow protégés were committed to the care of Warwick's 'Master of Henxmen', a household official whose duty it was to instil in Richard the rudiments of knightly conduct, described in the Household Book of Edward IV as 'the schools of urbanity and nurture of England'. He taught the henchmen to 'ride cleanly and surely; to draw them also to jousts; to learn them to wear their harness and to have all courtesy in words, deeds, and degrees' and 'diligently to keep them in the rules of goings and sittings'. The martial arts and good conduct in the company of his peers formed the basis of Richard's education but, like the traditional English public school education, it was also tempered with book learning and other liberal accomplishments. The Master of Henxmen

The great hall of Middleham Castle in Yorkshire, the favourite residence of Anne Beauchamp, Countess of Warwick. Middleham later became Richard's principal residence as Lieutenant of the North.

would teach his pupils 'sundry languages and other learning virtuous; to harp, to pipe, sing, dance with other temperate behaving'. The favourite popular reading of the time, prized for their moral as well as entertainment value, were the traditional tales of medieval chivalry. As William Caxton wrote later, 'read the noble volumes of Saint Grail, of Lancelot, of Galahad, of Tristram, of Perceforest, of Parseval, of Gawain and many more. There ye shall see manhood, courtesy, gentleness.' Richard never had the opportunity to read the greatest of all these epics: Sir Thomas Mallory's *Morte d'Arthur* was published three weeks before Bosworth.

When he was not out hunting with hawks and hounds in the Yorkshire dales or practising with sword and lance in the tilt yard, Richard's life centred around the communal routine of the Great Hall, presided over by the Countess and supervised by the Steward of the Household. Having risen shortly after dawn, he would repair here for dinner, the main meal of the day, at eleven. The whole of the 'standing' household – some two hundred persons in the case of a great earl like Warwick – would be present, seated at tables according to rank, and would gnaw their way through six whole oxen in a single day. Richard would again be on his best behaviour for 'this master [of Henchmen] sitteth in the Hall, next unto these henchmen, to have his respects unto their demeanings, how mannerly they eat and drink and to their communication and other forms curial [courtly], after the book of urbanity'. Supper was at five, followed by a couple of hours of relaxation and then bed. In the winter months the servants would distribute a livery of candles and firewood to heat the upper chambers.

In common with most castles erected before the fifteenth century, Middleham was a cold and draughty place, built to withstand siege rather than to offer domestic comforts. Newly wealthy knights and barons might rebuild in brick or timber as at Hurstmonceux and Tattershall, Crowhurst Place and Ockwells, but the blue-blooded had to make do with modern improvements – painted glass in the windows, and tapestries richly emblazoned with hunting scenes or heraldic devices on the walls – to brighten the stone relics of their ancestors.

Richard's companions at this time included some who were to play important roles in his future. Two fellow henchmen – Francis Lovell and Robert Percy – would remain his friends for life. About the same age as Richard was the Countess's elder daughter, Isabel, who would marry his brother George of Clarence. The younger daughter, Anne, would one day sit at Richard's side as Queen of England.

* * *

During these four years of Richard's schooling the great Earl of Warwick was too busy fighting on the king's behalf to spend much time at Middleham. Steel-willed in adversity, Queen Margaret and her Scottish allies hammered repeatedly at Edward's northern frontiers. Warwick, with his brother John, Lord Montagu, was equally tireless in defence. Three times the Lancastrians invaded Northumberland and three times they were beaten back with heavy losses. The differences in character that finally destroyed the partnership between the Earl and the young King were already apparent in their methods. Where Warwick proffered a mailed fist, Edward held out a velvet glove. His willingness to forgive and forget, his attempts to charm his enemies into submission, were a powerful boost to his popularity. But the men who returned his generosity with treason paid for it with their lives. In February 1462 John de Vere, 12th Earl of Oxford and his eldest son, Aubrey, were executed after the discovery of a plot to assassinate the king.

A more potent menace was Henry Beaufort, Duke of Somerset – the eldest son and heir of York's great enemy – whom Edward singled out as a special target for his charm. In the autumn of 1463 Edward planned a visit to Yorkshire to 'see and understand the disposition of the people of the North'. He took with him the Duke of Somerset and a bodyguard of 200 of Somerset's men 'well horsed and well harnessed'. On the way the citizens of Northampton, horrified to see their King apparently at the mercy of his hereditary foe, 'arose upon that false traitor the Duke of Somerset, and would have slain him within the king's palace. And then the king with fair speech and great difficulty saved his life for that time.... And the king full lovingly gave the Commons of Northampton a tun of wine that they should drink and make merry.' But the instincts of Edward's would-be rescuers proved correct. At the end of the year the Duke slipped away and organised a last ditch Lancastrian resistance from the Northumberland castle of Bamburgh. Again it was the Neville family who bailed Edward out from the consequences of his leniency. Outside Hexham on 14 May 1464, the Lancastrian rebels were soundly trounced by Lord Montagu. Somerset and his supporters were beheaded.

This battle virtually put an end to Lancastrian resistance. Shortly afterwards the Nevilles negotiated a fifteen-year-truce with the Scots and sealed the back door to Edward's kingdom. Warwick recaptured the three border strongholds of Alnwick, Dunstanburgh and Bamburgh – which had changed hands four times in as many years. Even Queen Margaret was momentarily subdued by this string of disasters; she retired at last to her father, René of Anjou's provincial Court at St Michel-sur-Bar. Sir John Fortescue described her little circle eking out a bitter Christmas in 1464: 'we beeth all in great poverty, but yet the Queen sustaineth us in meat and drink, so as we beeth not in extreme necessity... spend sparcely such money as ye have, for when ye come hither, ye shall have need of it'. Finally, in July 1465, Henry VI was tracked down to a Lancashire manor house and taken prisoner. With

his feet tied to the stirrups, he rode through London as Warwick's captive to take up residence in the Tower.

If Edward's throne was now secure, he owed a heavy debt to his two cousins, the Earl of Warwick and his brother John, Lord Montagu. The victor of Mortimer's Cross and Towton had already shown signs of preferring the pleasures of food and drink and pretty girls to the rigours of a campaign in the saddle. The Bishop of St Andrews rightly referred to the all-powerful Earl as the 'conductor of the kingdom under King Edward'. While Edward was content to take the advice of his mentor, Warwick had no reason to complain. After his victory at Hexham Lord Montagu was invested with the rich earldom of Northumberland and Warwick's clerical brother George, already Chancellor of England, was elevated to the archbishopric of York.

However, by the time the twelve-year-old Richard had been reunited with his brother at Court in the spring of 1465, the seeds of discord had been sown. In the previous autumn, at a Great Council convened at Reading,

Illustration from a law treatise of Henry VI's reign, showing the Court of the King's Bench at Westminster. At the top sit five presiding judges, and below them the King's Attorney, the Coroner and Masters of the Court, wearing party-coloured gowns of blue, and white, murrey and green. Standing on the green baized table are two ushers, one addressing the Court and the other administering an oath on the gospel to the jury. A prisoner stands in fetters at the bar in the custody of the marshal or tipstaff flanked by sergeants. Six more prisoners are shown in the foreground in the custody of tipstaffs.

Edward confronted a stunned assembly with the *fait accompli* of his secret marriage to Elizabeth Woodville. The circumstances in which this marriage took place were later recorded by Robert Fabyan:

> In such pass time, in most secret manner, upon the first day of May, King Edward spoused Elizabeth, late the wife of Sir John Grey, knight, which before time was slain at Towton or York Field, which spousals were solemnised early in the morning at a town named Grafton, near Stony Stratford; at which marriage was no persons present but the spouse, the spousess, the duchess of Bedford her mother, the priest, two gentlewomen, and a young man to help the priest sing. After which spousals ended, he went to bed, and so tarried there upon three or four hours....

Elizabeth, considering herself too good to become the king's whore, had the guts to turn down his advances and, like Anne Boleyn in the succeeding century, her scruples were rewarded with a Crown.

By any standards it was an amazingly tactless union. The Yorkist Queen was the widow of a Lancastrian knight, Sir John Grey, with two children of the same age as Edward's brothers. Far more important was the fact that it scotched the delicate negotiations that Warwick had set in motion for a marriage alliance with Europe's master diplomatist, King Louis XI of France. Such a match had obvious advantages for both parties. Edward's marriage to a French princess would knock away the last prop of Queen Margaret's hopes, and leave the king of France free to swallow up the two great ducal fiefs of Brittany and Burgundy. No family in England was more appreciative of the benefits of an advantageous match than the House of Neville, and Warwick rightly regarded the king's marriage as an affair of State rather than of the heart.

It rapidly became apparent that the Queen's relatives were no sluggards either when it came to playing the marriage game. Within fifteen months of Edward's revelation at Reading, the Earl of Arundel's heir, Lord Herbert's heir, and the twelve-year-old Duke of Buckingham were snapped up by three of the Queen's sisters, and one of her sons had taken the Duke of Exeter's heiress to the altar. The most notorious match was reserved for Elizabeth's brother John: in the words of a contemporary chronicler, 'Catherine, Duchess of Norfolk, a slip of a girl of about eighty years old, was married to John Wydeville, the Queen's brother, aged twenty years; a diabolical marriage.' To give Warwick his due, he was less upset by the advancement of the fecund Woodvilles than by the more basic differences in foreign policy that the marriage revealed. He himself escorted Elizabeth into the abbey chapel at Reading for her ceremonial recognition as Queen of England, and, according to one source close

The Schools of Urbanity and Nurture

Richard, Duke of Gloucester was taught the rudiments of knightly conduct in the Kingmaker's household at Middleham. Warwick's 'Master of Henxman' taught Richard and his friends to ride, to joust and to fight, and also supervised their book learning and reading.

ABOVE Chaucer's knight 'that from the time that he began to ride out, he loved chivalry, truth and honor', from the Prologue to the *Canterbury Tales*. This woodcut illustration is taken from Caxton's printed edition of the Tales.

OPPOSITE Miniature from the *Ordinances of Chivalry*, which was written for Sir John Astley before 1486. This shows a knight donning his tilting armour in his 'hut', which has been specially erected close to the jousting arena.

How a man schall be armyd at his ese
when he schal fighte on foote

He schal have noo schurte up on him but a dowbelet of ffustean lynyd with satene cutte full of hoolis. the dowbelet muste be strongeli bonde there the poyntis muste be sette aboute the greet of the arme. and the b ste before and behynde and the gussetis of mayle muste be sowid vn to the dowbelet in the bought of the arme. and vndir the arme the armynge poyntis muste be made of fyne twyne suche as men make stryngis for crossebowes and they to the Court, 'the Earl continued to show favour to the Queen's kindred, until he found that her relatives and connections... were using their utmost endeavours to promote the other marriage, which in conformity with the king's wishes eventually took place between Charles [of Burgundy] and the Lady Margaret [Edward's sister]'.

The Woodville affair could be pardoned as an indiscretion, but Edward's plan to ally England with Burgundy was in direct contradiction to his own plans for a *rapprochement* with France. It rapidly dawned on Warwick that Edward was no longer his protégé. Affable as ever, the king avoided a direct confrontation with the Earl, but, while Warwick continued his negotiations with Louis, Edward calmly pressed on with his own plans. For a time it seemed as if England had two masters, each bent on his own course. In the spring of 1467 two rival embassies visited Westminster, headed by the Bastard of Bourbon for France, and the Bastard of Burgundy for his master, each dangling marriage treaties and trade agreements. Sir John Paston wagered three marks that Philip of Burgundy's son Charles would not marry Margaret within two years. But Edward had his way, and the marriage treaty was finally ratified in March 1468.

Edward's preference for Burgundy was not just a whim designed to show his independence of the Earl. Edward still called himself King of France. Memories of the Hundred Years' War were fresh in English minds and Louis had lent Margaret his most able general to reconquer the Crown for Lancaster. He had good reason to suspect that Louis's friendship could prove as dangerous as his enmity. Burgundy, on the other hand, was England's traditional ally and trading partner, and Duke Philip had shown his friendship in 1461 by sheltering the Yorkist refugees.

Warwick did not take his defeat lightly. In June 1468, as he rode with Edward, George of Clarence and Richard of Gloucester to escort the future Duchess of Burgundy on her bridal journey to Margate, a new scheme was already half formed in his mind. The Nevilles had made one King: why not another? Edward had betrayed his trust, but his brother Clarence might prove more easily led – particularly if he was married to Warwick's nubile fifteen-year-old daughter Isabel. Edward had already incurred Clarence's resentment by vetoing this particular match, and other Yorkist magnates might well lend a hand if Warwick's *coup* promised an end to the ambitions of the voracious Woodvilles.

From the summer of 1468 to the spring of 1469 an uneasy truce prevailed as Warwick's plan matured. The country at large was well aware of the Earl's disaffection and particularly of his contempt for the Woodvilles. Robert Fabyan reported that

> ...many murmerous tales ran in the city atween th'earl of Warwick and the queen's blood, the which earl was ever had in great favour of the commons

> of this land, by reason of the exceeding household which he daily kept in all countries wherever he sojourned or lay, and when he came to London he held such an house that six oxen were eaten at breakfast, and every tavern was full of his meat, for who that had any acquaintance in that house, he should have had as much sodden and roast as he might carry upon a long dagger.

Edward's troubles began, early in 1469, with a series of mysterious risings in the North and Midlands, inspired by a rebel who called himself Robin of Redesdale. The size of Robin's army and the anti-Woodville slant of his proclamations were clear signs that he enjoyed the support of a more powerful backer. Somebody was also spreading the rumour that Edward was a bastard, in which event not he but George, Duke of Clarence, was rightfully King of England. In June Edward, accompanied by the Duke of Gloucester, set out to investigate the risings. Unaware that real danger threatened, he took with him only a small army and dawdled on the way. As soon as the king was safely out of reach, Warwick and Clarence slipped across the Channel to Calais and on 11 July George Neville, the Archbishop of York, officiated at Clarence's marriage to Isabel Neville. In the meantime Edward had realised that Robin of Redesdale's army was very much larger than his own and had fallen back on Nottingham. Warwick recrossed the Channel and marched north to join forces with Robin's men. Edward sat tight waiting for a relieving force under William Herbert, Earl of Pembroke, to join him at Nottingham. On 26 July, however, Pembroke's troops were crushed between the two rebel armies of Robin and Warwick near Banbury and cut to pieces. After writing a farewell note to his Woodville wife, Pembroke himself was executed at Warwick's orders: 'wife, pray for me and take the said order [of widowhood] that ye promised me, as ye had in my life my heart and love'.

Edward was completely outmanoeuvred. He now faced the choice of plunging the whole country into renewed anarchy or total surrender. The course he took revealed him as a master of political strategy. He dispersed his army, allowed the Woodvilles to scatter for cover, and calmly awaited his captors. Gambling on the assumption that Warwick would not dare have him killed, he knew that public sympathy would rally to him as the news of Warwick's treachery spread through the country. Within a few months the kingmaking Earl found himself at an *impasse*. His rebellion had sparked off a chain of minor disturbances that he could not put down without the king's authority. Even Warwick's brother John, the newly created Earl of Northumberland, refused to co-operate. By the end of September Edward was in a position to summon his supporters to his prison at Pontefract, and return to London with George Neville, his episcopal gaoler, trailing disconsolately behind him. 'Peace and entire oblivion of all grievances upon both sides was agreed to. Still, however, there probably remained, on the one side, deeply seated in his mind, the injuries he had received and the contempt which had been shown to majesty, and on the other: "A mind too conscious of a daring deed'" (Croyland Chronicle).

* * *

Edward's bloodless counter-coup marks an important stage in the career of his youngest brother Richard, Duke of Gloucester, now just celebrating his seventeenth birthday. In the years between leaving Middleham and Warwick's rebellion, we catch only a few brief glimpses of him. In 1466 he attended the installation of George Neville as Archbishop of York, and sat at table with the ladies at the sumptuous banquet that followed. Warwick himself served as steward. The menu, which represented the labours of 62 cooks, included 104 oxen, 6 wild bulls, 4,000 sheep, calves and pigs, 500 stags and 400 swans, and was washed down with 300 tuns of ale and 100 of wine. As a *pièce de résistance* the guests demolished a marzipan sculpture of St George lancing the dragon.

In February of 1467 Richard's name was joined with Warwick's and Northumberland's in a legal commission to hear cases at York: in June 1468, he is mentioned again as a member of his sister Margaret's nuptial train on its way to Margate. But it was in 1469 that his adolescence ended, and he was called to take up offices that held more than mere ceremonial significance. The events of that summer showed that Richard, despite his close association with the Nevilles, was deaf to the blandishments that had seduced his brother Clarence. Shortly after Edward's return to London the seventeen-year-old Duke of Gloucester was appointed Constable of England, and received a generous grant of land, including the castle of Sudeley in Gloucestershire. An uprising in Wales provided him with his first independent military command. Under his leadership the rebel-held strongholds of Carmarthen and Cardigan were retaken before the year's end. In the spring of 1470 Richard was further rewarded with numerous grants and offices that conferred on him wide authority throughout Wales.

The Welsh rising, however, was a sideshow: in the early spring of 1470 it was still the Earl of Warwick who occupied the centre of the political stage. No one could seriously have expected his formal reconciliation with the king to offer anything more than a breathing space. During Edward's captivity he had put to death the Queen's father, Earl Rivers, and one of her brothers at Warwick Castle. This act, even more than his rebellion, committed him to try again, if only to save his own neck from Queen Elizabeth's vengeance.

In February rebellion raised its head again in Lincolnshire. Its leaders, Lord Welles and Sir Thomas Dymmock, were quickly brought to heel by promises of a royal pardon, but Welles's son, Sir Robert, remained at large, defying the king in the name of the Duke of Clarence and the Earl of Warwick. By 12 March Edward's army was at Stamford, only a few miles from Sir Robert's forces. Warwick and Clarence were on their way from Coventry, ostensibly to help the king. But, before Warwick could join his forces to either side, the Lincolnshire rebels were put to flight at the battle known as Lose-Coat Field, and Sir Robert was a prisoner in Edward's hands. Sir Robert's confession confirmed the king's suspicions: the rising had been Warwick's work.

His treason unmasked and his Lincolnshire allies routed, Warwick cast about for other allies, first his own brother the Earl of Northumberland, then the Lancashire magnate Lord Stanley. Both turned a deaf ear. With the wretched Clarence still in tow, he fled south to the Devon coast and there boarded a ship for France. It was time to cash in on his friendship with King Louis. Embarrassed at first by the arrival of these uninvited guests, Louis soon rallied to evolve a scheme worthy of his diplomatic talents. If he could team up the fugitive Yorkist Earl with the exiled Lancastrian Queen in a successful bid to unseat King Edward, he would not only have his peace with England but also sever the English alliance with Burgundy. The reconciliation of two such bitter enemies was a formidable challenge to Louis's powers of persuasion: 'the queen was right difficile and showed to the king of France... that with the honour of her and her son, he nor she might not, nor could not pardon the said

Earl, which hath been the greatest causes of the fall of King Henry'. Nevertheless, Margaret's thirst for revenge on the House of York overcame her loathing for Warwick and, on 22 July 1470, she formally accepted his submission at the cathedral of Angers. Three days later the pact was sealed with the betrothal of the Queen's sixteen-year-old son, Edward, to Warwick's younger daughter, the fifteen-year-old Anne Neville. The Duke of Clarence, a willing enough stooge in his time, was quietly jettisoned with the promise that he would succeed to the throne if Edward and Anne failed to produce an heir.

Warwick's landing in Devon on 13 September was well timed, since it caught Edward in the north of his kingdom. Already accompanied by John de Vere, 13th Earl of Oxford and by Jasper Tudor, the kingmaker was soon joined by John Talbot, 3rd Earl of Shrewsbury and Lord Stanley. But once again there was to be no battle, thanks to another important defection from Edward's camp. Earlier in the year the king had tried to reconcile the powerful Lancastrian Percy family by restoring to it the earldom of Northumberland, which he had earlier bestowed on John Neville. In return John was asked to make do with the marquisate of Montagu. In response to this imagined slight the Marquess now decided to throw his lot in with his brother Warwick and almost succeeded in capturing the king at Doncaster. In the nick of time Edward rode away with a small band that included his brother Richard, his brother-in-law Anthony, Earl Rivers, and his Chamberlain, Lord Hastings. He commandeered a flotilla of fishing boats at the East Anglian port of Lynn and sailed for Burgundy. In London King Henry VI was hastily released from the Tower – 'not so cleanly kept as should seem such a Prince' – and dressed up in a blue velvet gown to receive the Kingmaker's homage. In the following month Edward's Queen Elizabeth gave birth to her first baby boy, Edward, in the Sanctuary of Westminster Abbey, where her husband's flight had compelled her to take refuge.

Edward and Richard were now the guests of Charles the Rash – ruler of Burgundy since Duke Philip's death in 1467 – and his Duchess, their sister Margaret. Charles was at first reluctant to become embroiled in the dynastic politics of his wife's family, but underwent a rapid conversion when King Louis declared war on him at Christmas. He realised that his duchy would not long survive an alliance between the French King and England's new master, the Earl of Warwick. On 11 March 1471 the Yorkists sailed from Flushing with a mixed army of Burgundians and Englishmen in a fleet of fourteen ships provided by the German merchants of the Hanse towns. Rebuffed in Norfolk and scattered by a storm off the Yorkshire coast, Edward's fleet at last made landfall on the Humber estuary. At this stage his meagre force of 1,600 men lay at the mercy of the Marquess Montagu and the Earl of Northumberland who each commanded superior forces in the vicinity. But both held back, content for the moment to let others decide the issue. Edward marched south unmolested, gathering recruits to his standard at Nottingham and Leicester. By 29 March he was outside Coventry, offering battle to his arch-enemy the Earl of Warwick. The kingmaker refused to leave the shelter of the city walls until he could be reinforced by the three converging armies of Montagu, Oxford and Clarence. It seemed as if his brash Yorkist cousin would soon be overwhelmed by superior numbers or sent packing back to Burgundy.

But Edward had an ace up his sleeve. During the winter of his exile 'great and diligent labour, with all effect, was continually made by the high and mighty princess, the duchess of Burgogne, which at no season ceased to send her servants, and messengers, to the king, where he was, and to my said Lord of Clarence, into England'; through the good offices of his sister Margaret, Clarence was duly persuaded to return to the fold. On 4 April the three brothers met outside Warwick. Clarence went down on his knees and made a formal submission to the king. A more tangible asset was the force of 4,000 men that Clarence brought with him to swell the Yorkist army.

With Warwick still bottled up in Coventry refusing to come out and fight, Edward decided to march on London. The defence of the capital had been entrusted to George Neville, the Archbishop of York, who also had charge of Henry VI. Robert Fabyan described his futile attempts to rally support in the solidly Yorkist city:

> And for to cause the citizens to bear their more favour unto King Henry, the said King Henry was conveyed from the palace of Paul's through Cheap and Cornhill, and so about to his said lodging again by Candlewick Street and Watling Street, being accompanied with the archbishop of York which held him all that way by the hand... the which was more liker a play than the showing of a prince to win men's hearts, for by this mean he lost many and won none or right few, and ever he was shewed in a long blue gown of velvet as though he had no moo to change with.

On 11 April Edward and Richard entered London to rapturous applause.

Edward's hold on London was one of the keys to his ultimate triumph over the House of Lancaster. Louis XI's adviser, Philip de Commynes, rather frivolously suggested that he owed his support to the gratitude of the burghers' wives whom he had selected to share his bed. But, apart from his emotional appeal, Edward had always fostered the interest of the merchant community, even to the extent of undertaking a number of commercial ventures on his own account. Unlike Henry VI in his single blue velvet gown, Edward was a big spender with a lot of unsettled bills to his name.

* * *

After a brief reunion with his wife and mother at Baynard's Castle and a first glimpse of his six-month-old son, Edward led his army out of London on the road to Barnet. For on Easter Saturday he heard the welcome news that Warwick had just passed through St Albans. Why was he now ready to give battle when he had refused Edward's challenge at Coventry? Queen Margaret was expected to land any day in Devon where John Courtenay, Earl of Devon and Edmund Beaufort, Duke of Somerset, were already levying troops in her name. Most probably he felt that his own position, already jeopardised by Clarence's defection, must be retrieved by a glorious victory won without the Queen's assistance.

Edward's outriders galloped into Barnet village that same afternoon, putting Warwick's scouts to flight. Half a mile beyond, they collided with the Earl's front line drawn up across a low ridge well shielded by hedgerows. Richard, who led the Yorkist van, conferred with his brother and despite the failing light they decided to press on beyond the village and take up their positions right under Warwick's nose. All night long Warwick's cannon pounded into the darkness. 'But', recorded an eye witness, 'thanked be God! it so fortuned that they alway overshot the king's host, and hurted them nothing.'

At daybreak on Easter Sunday both armies were obscured from each other's sight by a thick fog. Unbeknown to Edward the two lines of battle overlapped; his left, under Lord Hastings, was outflanked by Warwick's right under the Earl of Oxford, while the Yorkist right, commanded by Richard, outflanked the Duke of Exeter's men on the Lancastrian left. As soon as the fighting began, Hastings was in trouble. Under heavy pressure both from the front and on the flank his troops wavered, fell back and finally broke. With Oxford's men at their heels, they abandoned the field and streamed back down the road towards London. By mid-morning the streets of the capital were alive with rumours that 'the king was distressed and his field lost'. At the same time Richard was taking advantage of his corresponding overlap on the right, so weakening Exeter's flank that Warwick had to commit the Lancastrian reserves.

Edward, commanding the Yorkist centre, was now in great danger from Oxford's victorious troops. Returning from the rout of Hastings's men, Oxford intended to attack the king from the rear. But by now the line of battle had swung around from an east–west to a north–south axis, and the Earl of Oxford's men collided not with Edward's troops, but with Montagu's. Met by a volley of arrows from Montagu's archers, Oxford's men panicked and fell back. The Earl of Oxford himself fled from the field, convinced that Montagu had turned his coat again.

The ensuing confusion decided the day. By 7 a.m. the Lancastrian front was broken, and Montagu was dead. Warwick was overtaken in flight by the king's men and put to death on the spot. As proof of his decisive victory, Edward had the two Neville corpses exposed to public view at St Paul's.

On that same Easter Sunday, Queen Margaret landed at Weymouth with her son, Prince Edward. Bottled up by head winds at Honfleur for three weeks, she came too late to save the House of Neville. But the Duke of Somerset was quick to point out that Edward's army too had been badly mauled; in Wales and Lancashire, the traditional strongholds of her House, she could still bring enough men to her banners to reverse the verdict of Barnet. Speed was all important, for if Edward could hold or destroy the bridges on the River Severn before she could cross, Margaret would be cut off. On 3 May she reached the first crossing-point at Gloucester after an all-night march: but the gates were closed and Edward was by now too close behind to let her risk an assault on the town. Without pause she drove on to the next passage at Tewkesbury. Here, at four in the afternoon, she was compelled to rest. Her foot soldiers were exhausted and even the horses were flagging. Camping in a field outside the town that night, Margaret realised that she must now turn and fight.

On Saturday 4 May 1471, it was Richard, Duke of Gloucester who led the Yorkist van on the road from Cheltenham to Tewkesbury. This time he faced the Lancastrian left, commanded by Edmund Beaufort, Duke of Somerset, the third to bear that title in a cause that had already carried off his father and his elder brother. The ground between the two armies was a patchwork of 'foul lanes and deep dykes, and many hedges', well reconnoitred by Somerset's scouts but unfamiliar to Richard. Perceiving his advantage, Somerset marched his men swiftly round to Richard's flank and launched his attack.

It was a well-judged move, but Somerset knew nothing of the company of spearmen Edward had stationed in a wood a few hundred yards to the left of Richard's position. Those '200 spears' now found themselves ideally placed at Somerset's rear. Seizing their opportunity they 'came and brake on, all at once upon the Duke of Somerset and his vanguard... whereof they were greatly dismayed and abashed, and so took them to flight into the park, and into the meadow that was near, and into lanes and dykes, where they best hoped to escape the danger'. Richard's men surged forward and the pursuit became a rout. Somerset's retreat was cut off by the River Avon and the field across which he fled earned the name of Bloody Meadow.

Richard's success proved decisive. While Edward pressed the attack on the Lancastrian centre, Richard's men rounded on their unprotected flank. The entire

The Battle of Tewkesbury, 4 May 1471, when Edward IV crushed the Lancastrian forces of Margaret of Anjou. Many leading Lancastrians were killed in the battle, including the only son and heir of Margaret and Henry VI, Edward Prince of Wales.

Lancastrian line crumbled and fled. Prince Edward was overtaken by a detachment of Clarence's men and butchered. The rebel leaders who had taken sanctuary in Tewkesbury Abbey were dragged out, condemned and beheaded in the market place. A few days later Queen Margaret was taken prisoner and the last Lancastrian force in England – the Kentishmen raised by the Bastard of Fauconberg – retired from an abortive siege of London.

One last grisly act sealed the triumph of the House of York. In the words of the chronicler John Warkworth:

> And the same night that King Edward came to London, King Henry, being inward in prison in the Tower of London, was put to death, the 21st day of May, on a Tuesday night, between eleven and twelve of the clock, being then at the Tower the duke of Gloucester, brother to King Edward, and many other; and on the morrow he was chested and brought to Paul's, and his face was open that every man might see him; and in his lying he bled on the pavement there; and afterward at the Black Friars was brought, and there he bled new and fresh; and from thence he was carried to Chertsey Abbey in a boat, and buried there in our Lady Chapel.

3

‘Loyalty binds me’

1471–83

Edward's murder of the harmless, kindly and befogged King Henry shocked many of his contemporaries. In the words of the author of the Great Chronicle of London, Henry cared 'little or nothing of the pomp or vanities of this world, wherefore after my mind he might say, as Christ said to Pilate, "my kingdom is not of this world" for God had endowed him with such grace that he chose the life contemplative, the which he forsook not from his tender age unto the last day of his life'. Of his many acts of kindness, none is more poignant than the concern he showed for Edward's wife during her confinement in Westminster Abbey, when he sent her food and wine.

Yet Henry was the victim not of Edward's cruelty, but of his own saintly indifference to worldly affairs. He lost his throne because England needed a king, not a monk – a strong king who could restore order, dispense justice and promote trade. He lost his life because the magic of his name could still inspire the respect and loyalty that men like Warwick needed to mask their cynical ambitions. With Henry as a focus for the plots, uprisings and invasions that blighted the early promise of Edward's reign, the monarchy tumbled into disrespect and the Crown became no more than first prize in an aristocratic power game. As the chronicler John Warkworth shrewdly noted 'When King Edward reigned, the people looked after all the aforesaid prosperities and peace, but it came not; but one battle after another, and much trouble and great loss of goods among the common people.' Henry, the guiltless cause of so much trouble, had to die so that the king could be king.

A later generation of Tudor historians, brought up on tales of Richard's villainy, could not resist the imputation that Richard was personally responsible for the deaths of both Henry VI and his son Edward. According to Edward Hall, who wrote in Henry VIII's reign, Prince Edward was not slain at the Battle of Tewkesbury but taken prisoner and brought before the king, 'being a goodly feminine and well featured young gentleman'. Whereupon the king:

> ...demanded of him, how he durst so presumptuously enter into his Realm with banner displayed. The prince, being bold of stomach and of a good courage, answered saying: to recover my father's kingdom and inheritage.... At which words King Edward said nothing, but with his hand thrust him from him (or, as some say, stroke him with his gauntlet), whom incontinent, they that stood about which were George, Duke of Clarence, Richard, Duke of Gloucester, Thomas, Marquess Dorset and William, Lord Hastings, suddenly murdered and piteously manquelled.

Of Henry VI's death the same author writes: 'Poor King Henry the Sixth, a little before deprived of his realm and imperial crown was now in the Tower of London spoiled of his life... by Richard Duke of Gloucester (as the constant fame ran) which to the intent that King Edward his brother should be clear of all secret suspicion of sudden invasion, murdered the said king with a dagger.' In fact, there is no foundation for either of these stories. All the contemporary accounts of Tewkesbury, Lancastrian and Yorkist, simply state that Prince Edward was slain on the battlefield. Likewise, all that is known of Henry's murder is the bald fact of his death, along with Warkworth's statement that Richard accompanied his brothers 'and many others' to the Tower on the fatal night.

The Duke of Gloucester was, however, to play a vital part in restoring the majesty of the Crown. In July 1471 – only a few weeks after the exhausting ordeal of the Tewkesbury campaign – he was on his way north to deal with a new rash of border incidents on the Scottish Marches. This was no temporary commission. Edward had decided to invest the eighteen-year-old veteran of his two great victories with the spoils – and the responsibilities – of the conquered Earl of Warwick.

In the northern counties and the Scottish Marches a strong tradition of lawlessness and independence defied the efforts of the distant Council at Westminster to impose order and justice. The rugged and backward North had long enjoyed a political complexion different from that of the South. In order to protect the border against Scottish incursions, successive English kings had invested great families, such as the Nevilles and the Percies, with huge estates and semi-regal powers to raise private armies as Wardens of the Marches. For fifteen years, the open warfare between the Nevilles and Percies had promoted local feuds and invited the depredations of the Scots.

With the extinction of the House of Lancaster and the disgrace of the Nevilles, only one great magnate was left in the North. Edward had restored Henry Percy, barely in his twenties, to the earldom of Northumberland in 1470. The last four generations of Percies had died in civil wars, the last two in the Lancastrian cause. Clearly the time had come to appoint a strong man who could both fill the vacuum left by the Nevilles, and balance the dubious loyalty of the young Earl of Northumberland. Richard's headquarters were to be at the familiar castle of Middleham, which was granted to him along with the former Neville lordships of Sheriff Hutton and Penrith, and the whole of Warwick's holdings in Yorkshire and Cumberland. Two important offices further buttressed his power: the stewardship of the duchy of Lancaster beyond the Trent, and the wardenship of the West Marches towards Scotland, with final authority over Henry Percy, who was Warden of the Middle and Eastern Marches. His former Welsh offices were, in the meantime, transferred to the young William Herbert, Earl of Pembroke (later Earl of Huntingdon).

The summer months passed as Richard reviewed his new estates and conducted a short foray against the

Scottish border raiders, but in the autumn he hurried back to London on family business. Prior to his departure Richard had sought and obtained the king's permission to marry Anne Neville. Only sixteen years old, the kingmaker's daughter was already the fatherless widow of a Prince, although it is unlikely that the marriage was ever consummated. From Richard's point of view the young cousin who had watched him learn to hunt and joust at Middleham was an ideal bride. The marriage would discharge a debt of honour to the family that had taken him into their household. On a material level, it would confirm him in his title to Warwick's northern possessions, and bring him a share of the even more extensive Beauchamp estates that Warwick had held in his wife's right.

It was the question of Anne's inheritance that now sparked off an ugly quarrel with Clarence. As the husband of Warwick's elder daughter, Isabel, Clarence had hoped to appropriate the whole of the Beauchamp lands, which belonged properly to his mother-in-law, Anne Beauchamp. Even this princely inheritance – more than one hundred and fifty manors scattered throughout the country from Devon to Durham – was a meagre consolation for the crown Clarence dreamed of wearing, and he did not intend to share it with his younger brother.

When Richard arrived at Clarence's lodgings to claim his prospective bride, he was told to keep his hands off her. Richard appealed to the king, who ordered Clarence not to interfere with the proposed marriage. Clarence retaliated by persuading Anne to dress up as a kitchen maid, and concealed her in the household of a friend. Like most of Clarence's schemes, the ruse was soon uncovered, and Richard had her removed to the sanctuary of St Martin's. At this point the king intervened to mediate between the brothers before the affair got out of hand. Both put their case at a Council meeting, where even the lawyers were surprised by the subtlety of their arguments. In point of fact, Clarence had no case at all: he was not Anne's guardian in any legal sense, and the girl's mother was still alive, immured in the sanctuary of Beaulieu Abbey since the Battle of Tewkesbury. Nevertheless, Edward found it politic to soothe Clarence's ruffled feathers and a compromise was reached. Richard's marriage was to go ahead, but he was to receive only a part of Warwick's personal holdings, while the rest, including the Countess's inheritance and the earldoms of Warwick and Salisbury, was reserved for Clarence. In addition, Richard was induced to give up to Clarence his office of Great Chamberlain.

Although Anne and Richard were cousins, the marriage was quickly celebrated without the formality of a papal dispensation, and the couple retired to Yorkshire. Early in 1473 the Duchess of Gloucester gave birth to a son who was christened Edward. Four months later Richard persuaded the king – despite vehement protests from

Clarence – to allow his mother-in-law to leave sanctuary unharmed and to join the household at Middleham.

The Clarence-Gloucester quarrel exhibits all the worst features of a private baronial feud blown up into a threat to public order by the irresponsible behaviour of those involved. Richard's considerate treatment of the Countess of Warwick and his subsequent attempts to obtain a pardon for George Neville, the Archbishop of York, show that his motives, at least, were tempered by some concern for the family under whose roof he had grown up at Middleham. But it is hard to find any redeeming features in Clarence's behaviour. He was bent on making trouble, even though he had acquired the lion's share of the Warwick inheritance. In 1472 and 1473 rumours again linked his name with Louis XI, who sponsored an unsuccessful invasion led by that most tenacious of all Lancastrian supporters, the Earl of Oxford. When the Earl landed at St Michael's Mount in late September 1473, Clarence was breathing dark hints of treason and vengeance. In London Sir John Paston reported that the king's entourage sent for their harness to prepare for the worst: 'the Duke of Clarence maketh himself big in that he can, showing as he would but deal with the Duke of Gloucester. But the king intendeth to be as big as they both and to be a stifler between them. And some think that under this there be some other thing intended, and some treason conspired.'

The crisis was happily averted – or at least postponed –

by the failure of Oxford's attempted invasion. He never got further than St Michael's Mount, where he was bottled up until Edward induced him to surrender in February 1474. Clarence was not called to account for his treasonable posturings: the king patiently agreed to look into his grievances, and a fresh division of the Warwick estates was submitted to Parliament for approval.

The long-term consequences of this episode were by no means exhausted, but towards the end of 1474 a more important enterprise overshadowed the affairs of the kingdom. Edward IV had decided to settle accounts with Louis XI, and was preparing to lead an invasion of France in the following spring. Since 1461 Louis had sanctioned one attempt after another against the Yorkist throne: first, Margaret of Anjou's, then Warwick's and now Oxford's. Edward did not seriously contemplate the reconquest of a kingdom at least four times as populous as his own: but in concert with Louis's arch enemy, Charles, Duke of Burgundy, he could inflict a punishing blow that would restore England's initiative in foreign policy and avenge the endless humiliations of Henry VI's reign.

Edward's enterprise was first mooted in 1472, and Parliament had already voted a special tax to pay the wages of 13,000 archers. Efforts to collect this tax foundered on the stubborn resistance of 'the generality of his said commons', and the king was compelled to resort to the equally unpopular but more effective practice of raising benevolences. These loans-on-demand, voluntary in theory but difficult to refuse in practice, were begged or bullied from all men of substance – £30 from the Mayor of London, £10 – £20 from the Aldermen and £4 11s 3d, 'the wages of half a soldier for a year', from the head commoners. One merry widow from Suffolk was rewarded for her £10 by a royal kiss, and promptly doubled her contribution.

The army was raised by means of indenture – a contract whereby the principals bound themselves to supply an agreed number of men at an agreed fee. Richard, as the second man in the kingdom, indented for 120 mounted lances and 1,000 archers – about one-tenth of the host that embarked for Calais in June 1475. Louis's adviser, Philip de Commynes, described it as 'the most numerous, the best disciplined, the best mounted and the best armed that ever any king of that nation invaded France withal'. The French Court was close to panic: an Italian envoy reported that 'his Majesty is more discomposed than words can describe and has almost lost his wits. In his desperation and bitterness he uttered the following precise words, among others, Ah Holy Mary, even now when I have given thee 1,400 crowns, thou dost not help me one whit.'

Nevertheless, divine intervention was at hand. Twelve months previously the Duke of Burgundy had bound himself to join Edward with a force of 10,000 men not later than 1 July 1475. But for months past he had been embroiled in the schemes of his eastern neighbour, the Holy Roman Emperor, and when he finally presented himself on 14 July, his promised army was busy pillaging Lorraine. 'God,' as Commynes remarked, 'had troubled his sense and his understanding.'

Prospects of a second Agincourt were receding fast, and on 11 August they were blighted by a second disappointment. The Count of St Pol, who had promised Charles and Edward the important town of St Quentin, closed the gates and fired on the English as they advanced to take possession. On the same day the Duke of Burgundy took his leave, ostensibly to collect his army for an assault on Champagne. For Edward this was the last straw: the following day he opened negotiations with Louis. Too much of a realist to hope for the reconquest of Normandy and Guienne, Edward was quite prepared to let the threat of force extract concessions as favourable as any he might obtain on the battlefield. Louis also was a realist, and it took only three days to hammer out the main heads of agreement. For a down payment of 75,000 crowns and an annual subsidy of 50,000, Edward would take his army home again. English and French merchants were freed from trade restrictions in each other's countries. The five-year-old Dauphin was betrothed to Edward's ten-year-old-daughter Elizabeth. Margaret of Anjou, a prisoner since Tewkesbury, would be ransomed for a further 50,000 crowns. And both Kings promised to aid each other against rebellious subjects. Before the treaty was formally concluded on 29 August 1475 by the two sovereigns in person at Picquigny, Louis organised a gigantic alcoholic party for the entire English army at Amiens: it lasted three days.

There was, however, a minority who felt that Edward's peace treaty was no cause for celebration – among them the Duke of Gloucester. Richard was conspicuously absent from the signing ceremony: his sympathies were with the Gascon knight who told Commynes that Picquigny was a disgrace outweighing all King Edward's battle honours. Or, as Louis himself put it, 'I have chased the English out of France more easily than my father ever did; for my father drove them out by force of arms, whereas I have driven them out with venison pies and good wine.'

Who, in fact, gained most from the Peace of Picquigny? The speed with which terms were arranged suggests that both sides got what they wanted. Edward had made his point about Louis's meddling in English affairs, and received a handsome tribute for the privilege. Louis was left free to plot the destruction of Burgundy, and he could call the king of England his pensioner.

On 21 August Edward's army re-embarked for England and early in September Richard was back in Wensleydale. Here he spent the best part of the next two years. When he returned to the Court in February 1477 it was to face a new crisis in foreign policy – and the last act in the pitiful career of George, Duke of Clarence. The crisis arose from the death in the Battle of Nancy of Charles, Duke of Burgundy, at the hands of Swiss pikemen, on 1 January 1477. With him were slaughtered the remains of the Burgundian army, which had already sustained a crushing defeat at the Battle of Morat six months previously. King Louis, wrote Commynes, 'was so overjoyed he scarcely knew how to react'. This was an overstatement. Since Charles left no male heir, Louis immediately claimed that the duchy of Burgundy, along with the northern counties of Artois, Picardy and Flanders, reverted to the French Crown. His opponents were Charles's twenty-year-old daughter Mary, and her childless step-mother, Margaret of York.

Margaret naturally turned to her brother Edward for help. But Edward could not make up his mind. There was a strong case for propping up the shaky Burgundian régime, which had, in the past, provided a useful check to Louis's more extravagant ambitions. Should the Burgundian possessions in Flanders fall to the French Crown, England's continental foothold at Calais would be entirely surrounded by Louis's domains. But, if Edward declared openly in favour of Charles's heiress, he would have to forego his French pension and disburse the considerable treasure he had amassed since 1475 on an expeditionary force. In the end he made a few ineffectual protests and did nothing. Despairing of Edward's help, Mary's advisers scoured the courts of Europe for a rich and war-like husband to come to her rescue. An atmosphere of gloomy foreboding dominated the English Court. 'It seemeth that the world is all quavering', wrote John Paston, 'It will reboil somewhere, so that I deem young men shall be cherished.'

The young man the Dowager Duchess Margaret cherished was George, Duke of Clarence. Here was a golden chance to bestow on her favourite brother, whose wife had just died in childbirth, the hand of the greatest heiress in Europe. However, it was hardly surprising, as the Croyland Chronicler put it, that:

> ...so great a contemplated exaltation of his ungrateful brother displeased the king. He consequently threw all possible impediments in the way, in order that the match before-mentioned might not be carried into effect, and exerted all his influence that the heiress might be given in marriage to Maximilian [of Austria], the son of the [Holy Roman] Emperor; which was afterwards effected. The indignation of the Duke was probably still further increased by this; and now each began to look upon the other with no very fraternal eyes. You might then have seen (as such men are generally to be found in the courts of all princes), flatterers running to and fro, from the one side to the other, and carrying backwards and forwards the words which had fallen from the two brothers, even if they had happened to be spoken in the most secret closet.

Clarence's paranoid feelings were further inflamed by the news that Edward had proposed as his candidate for Mary's husband a member of the despised Woodville clan, the Queen's brother Anthony, Earl Rivers. This time Edward was not prepared to turn a deaf ear to his brother's threats of treason and revenge. After a final warning Clarence was to be struck down. The warning took the form of a death sentence on one of the Duke's retainers, one Thomas Burdett, who was condemned on charges of treasonable writing and necromancy. Ignoring the danger signal Clarence interrupted a Council meeting at Westminster to protest Burdett's innocence. Even more recklessly he began to spread the old story that Edward was a bastard, armed his retainers and managed to engineer riots in Cambridgeshire and Huntingdonshire. In the meantime, King Louis, ever anxious to keep his English cousins at each other's throats while he completed the dismemberment of Burgundy, sent word of further treasonable gossip. Edward summoned Clarence to Westminster and had him confined to the Tower.

There is no record that Richard had any part in these proceedings, and it seems likely that the summer months kept him busy in Yorkshire. When he rejoined the Court in the late autumn Clarence's life hung by a thread. The Woodvilles, who still regarded him as Warwick's accomplice in the murder of two of their kin, were baying for his blood, and the story of the king's bastardy was one that snapped even Edward's patience. Richard was the only member of the royal family to speak up for his brother: Clarence was a nuisance, but since Warwick's defeat he had never been a threat. Moreover, he was loath to see the Woodvilles manoeuvring one of his brothers into killing the other.

But Edward was determined to go through with it. On 16 January 1478, the Lords assembled in Parliament before the king to try Clarence on charges of high treason. In a hushed chamber none of them dared utter a word in accusation or defence. Only the king could prosecute the king's brother. The verdict was 'guilty', and the Duke of Buckingham, as Steward of England, pronounced the sentence of death. When Edward hesitated to set a date for the execution, the Commons presented a petition that it should be carried out swiftly. A few days later the Duke of Clarence at last earned in his death the fame that had eluded him in his lifetime, when he was drowned in a butt of Malmsey wine. Contemporary accounts record that Edward offered Clarence a choice of death, and that he elected to be drowned in a butt of wine. This has led later historians to declare that Clarence was a drunkard, but others have suggested that the butt of Malmsey held a symbolic significance as a reminder of the presents of tuns of wine sent to Clarence by Edward in happier days. Margaret Pole, Clarence's daughter, certainly wore a model of a wine cask on her wrist in remembrance of her father's death.

Dominic Mancini, the Italian cleric who in 1483 wrote an invaluable account of his stay in England, states that Richard was 'overcome with grief for his brother'. He also provides the clue to the origins of Richard's bitter antagonism towards the Woodvilles:

> Thenceforth [Mancini continues] Richard came very rarely to court. He kept himself within his own lands and set out to acquire the loyalty of his people through favours and justice. The good reputation of his private life and public activities powerfully attracted the esteem of strangers.... Such was his renown in warfare, that whenever a difficult and dangerous policy had to be undertaken, it would be entrusted to his discretion and his generalship. By these arts Richard acquired the favour of the people, and avoided the jealousy of the Queen, from whom he lived far separated.

* * *

Clarence's death clearly left scars on Richard's memory. Three days after the execution he procured a licence to set up two religious foundations to pray for the royal family and for his dead brothers and sisters. It is equally clear that he blamed the Woodville Queen for what had happened. But his estrangement from the Court went deeper than this. The reference to 'the good reputation of his private life' hints at a contrast between Richard's asceticism and the frivolity, the gormandising and the freewheeling sexual antics of Edward's entourage. The differences between the two surviving sons of York are so strong as to prompt the thought that there may have been some foundation for the tale of Edward's bastardy. Richard, short, frailly

built, intense and rather straight-laced, and ill at ease in company; Edward, a fat, pleasure-loving giant with easy manners and extravagant tastes. Mancini paints a striking portrait of Edward in his later years:

> In food and drink he was most immoderate: it was his habit, so I have learned, to take an emetic for the delight of gorging his stomach once more. For this reason and for the ease, which was especially dear to him after his recovery of the crown, he had grown fat in the loins, whereas previously he had been not only tall but rather lean and very active. He was licentious in the extreme: moreover it was said that he had been most insolent to numerous women after he had seduced them, for, as soon as he grew weary of dalliance, he gave up the ladies much against their will to the other courtiers. He pursued with no discrimination the married and unmarried, the noble and lowly: however he took none by force. He overcame all by money and promises, and having conquered them, he dismissed them. Although he had many promoters and companions of his vices, the more important and especial were three of the aforementioned relatives of the queen, her two sons and one of her brothers.

Although York Minster was commenced in the thirteenth century, it was not completed until the mid-fifteenth, when the western towers and central tower were added in the perpendicular style.

As Mancini points out, it was in the North, far removed from the Court's politics and pleasures, that Richard's talents were most fruitfully employed. *'Loyauté me lie'* – 'loyalty binds me' – was the motto Richard adopted, and for thirteen years he effectively ruled the northern counties as Edward's deputy in war and peace. His first task was to establish a working relationship with the Earl of Northumberland. Generations of Percies had been lords of the North, and much depended on Richard's tactful handling of the young Earl. In May 1473 the two men entered into a formal agreement, whereby Henry Percy recognised Richard's ultimate authority, while Richard promised to uphold the Earl's rights. In the East Riding and in Northumberland Percy's authority continued unchallenged: Westmorland, Cumberland and the West Riding were Richard's preserve.

The key to the North was York itself, a city of more than twelve thousand inhabitants, and headquarters of a prosperous merchant community. The Merchant Adventurers of York, incorporated more than a century before, carried on a brisk trade with the Hanse towns and supplied the city with its municipal officers. More than once discontented factions appealed to the Earl of Northumberland over Richard's head, but the city's records show that the great majority of the citizens regarded the Duke of Gloucester as their special friend and protector. The details of his administration confirm the importance that the Yorkist rulers attached to their relationships with the major cities of the realm – a fact often obscured by the battles, executions, feuds and intrigues that monopolised the attentions of the chroniclers. Authorising the destruction of illegal fish traps on the Humber and the Ouse, arbitrating in disputed municipal elections, quelling riots and commuting taxes in times of need, Richard worked hard to earn the title of 'our full tender and especial good lord'. A typical entry in the civic minutes records the decision that 'the Duke of Gloucester shall, for his great labour now late made unto the king's good grace for the confirmation of the liberties of this City be presented, at his coming to the City, with six swans and six pikes'. When the traditional spring pageant was celebrated in 1477 Richard and Anne marked their special bond with the city by joining the Corpus Christi Guild, a religious fraternity closely associated with the powerful Merchant Adventurers.

It was an active life that left Richard little time to enjoy the comforts of his Duchess's household at Middleham. When in York he generally stayed at the house of the Augustinian friars at Lendal. His estates at Sheriff Hutton, about ten miles north-east of the city, were also conveniently close and bordered on some of Henry Percy's chief manors. The castle of Pontefract, twenty-two miles to the south-west, was his official residence as Steward of the Duchy of Lancaster beyond Trent, while Barnard Castle, some fifty miles to the north-west, was his chief seat in the county of Durham. Richard's normal

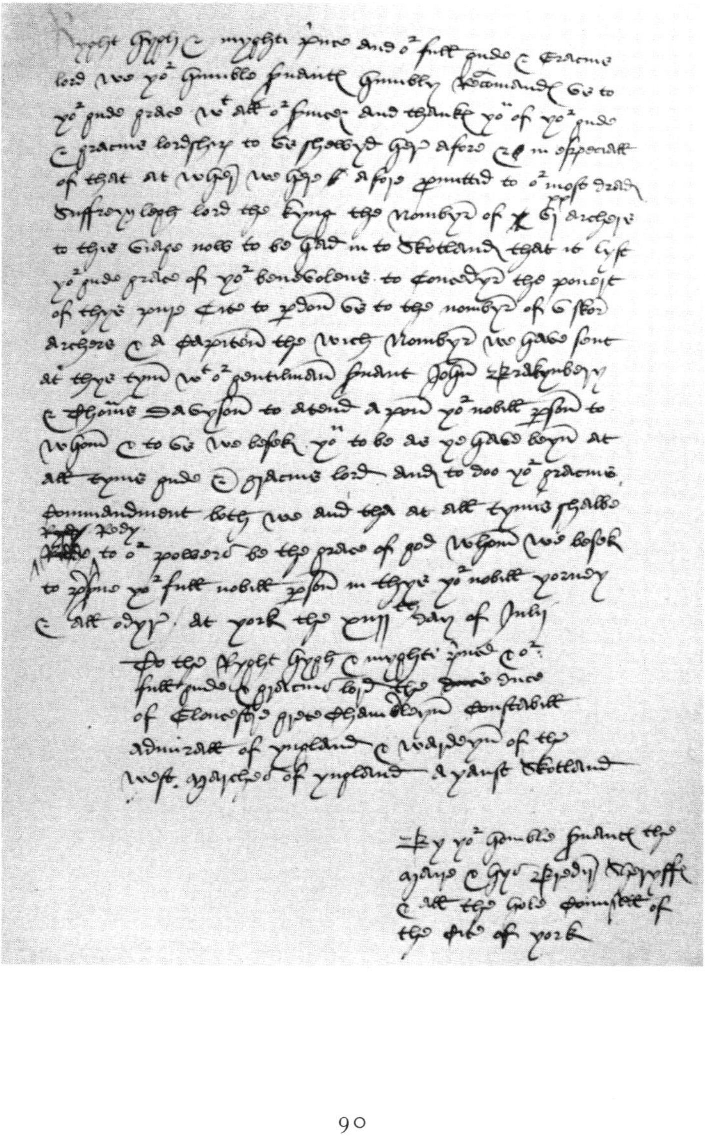

administrative duties were frequently supplemented by legal commissions that toured the countryside hearing pleas, initiating inquiries and settling disputes. As Richard's reputation spread, the personal following who comprised his Council took on increasingly the functions of a court of law, offering 'good and indifferent justice to all who sought it, were they rich or poor, gentle or simple'.

Richard's other great office, the wardenship of the West March, did not seriously occupy his attention until the spring of 1480. Persuading James III of Scotland to break his truce and authorise large-scale border raids was one of Louis's many ploys to keep the English busy while he tidied up his Burgundian conquests. In May Richard's military powers were augmented by the office of Lieutenant General in the North, and in the autumn of 1480 he launched a border raid of his own into Scottish territory. This was to be the curtain-raiser to a full scale invasion planned for the summer of 1481. King Edward was to command in person. With Northumberland as his deputy, Richard spent the winter inspecting the border garrisons, repairing the fortifications of Carlisle and conducting a military census. Late in March 1481 he was with Edward in London, putting the finishing touches to their plan of campaign.

Letter from the Mayor and Council of York, thanking Richard, Duke of Gloucester who, in consideration of the city's poverty, had reduced the number of men required for the campaign to Scotland by twenty archers and a captain.

But the campaign never materialised. Although a fleet under Lord Howard devastated Scottish shipping in the Firth of Forth, Edward never stirred from his capital, immobilised by financial worries and failing health. Richard and Northumberland were left to conduct a border raid on a scale no greater than that of the previous autumn. By the spring of 1482 a significant victory over the Scots had become a political as well as a military necessity. The exceptionally bad harvest of 1481 was causing severe disturbances in several counties; Edward's attempts to levy a tax, commuted on his return from the inglorious French campaign of 1475, proved as unpopular as benevolences; and there were rumours that Burgundy, despairing of armed support from England, was about to come to terms with King Louis. In that event England would be isolated without a continental ally, and Edward could kiss goodbye to his annual French pension.

In 1482 the sole command of the Scottish expedition was vested in the Duke of Gloucester. The two brothers met at Fotheringhay in June, and Richard was furnished with an unexpected ally in the person of James III's younger brother, the Duke of Albany – a 'Clarence in kilt' – whom the brothers promised to seat on James's throne. Early in July Richard and Northumberland marshalled their forces under the battlements of Alnwick Castle in Northumberland. The army was estimated at twenty thousand men, backed by a formidable siege train of artillery. Their first objective was the town of Berwick, in Scottish hands since Margaret had surrendered it two decades before. The town itself capitulated at once but the citadel, commanded by the Earl of Bothwell, held out. Detaching Lord Stanley and his contingent from Lancashire and Cheshire to press the siege, Richard drove on to meet the Scottish army. After all the efforts and expense that had gone into the campaign, it must have come as something of a disappointment to hear, at the end of July, that James III was the victim of a *coup* organised by his own barons. Disillusioned by their sovereign's foolhardy sabre-rattling, the Scottish lords refused to risk their lives in a pitched battle, and Richard entered Edinburgh unopposed. At Albany's request Richard's soldiers were forbidden even their traditional right to pillage the conquered city. Negotiations for a peace settlement proved equally fruitless: no treaty would long survive the political upheavals of James's Court. Mindful of the crippling costs of keeping his army in the field indefinitely, Richard had no alternative but to march back the way he had come, determined at least to salvage his and the nation's pride by completing the reduction of Berwick Castle. Albany, who had made his peace with the Scottish lords, remained behind, promising to secure a lasting truce for his English allies. On 24 August the Scots at last agreed to the permanent cession of Berwick to the English Crown, and the citadel was delivered to Lord Stanley. The news was trumpeted in London as if Richard had won a second Agincourt, and Edward was lavish in his praises. In a sour and more realistic vein, the Croyland Chronicler noted that 'this trifling, I know not whether to call it "gain" or "loss" (for the safekeeping of Berwick each year swallows up ten thousand marks) at this period diminished the resources of the king and kingdom by more than a hundred thousand pounds'.

The man who benefited most from Richard's martial exploits was undoubtedly 'the universal spider', Louis XI. For, shortly after Christmas, the Court learned that Maximilian and Mary of Burgundy had signed a treaty with the king of France. Their daughter Margaret was to marry the Dauphin, in flagrant disregard of the Dauphin's previous betrothal to Edward's daughter Elizabeth.

The collapse of Edward's diplomacy abroad did not touch Richard's reputation. In recognition of ten years and more of service in the North, capped by the subjection of Edinburgh and the recapture of Berwick, Parliament bestowed on him in February 1483 the permanent and hereditary wardenship of the West Marches towards Scotland. This plum was sugared with a further grant of the castle and city of Carlisle, and all the king's manors and revenues in the county of Cumberland. To these would be added any further conquests won from the Scots. At the age of thirty Richard could look forward to the undisputed possession of his own palatinate, and many years of active service in which to give rein to his proven talents.

4
The Usurper

April–July 1483

Richard's sojourn as lieutenant of the North was brought to an abrupt end by the death of Edward IV on 9 April 1483. Overweight and oversexed, his indulgence of these two appetites had undermined his health, but it was a chill caught on a fishing trip that was reported to have killed him. He left his kingdom and his Crown to his twelve-year-old son Edward, Prince of Wales, who kept his own Court at Ludlow Castle under the care of his uncle Anthony, Earl Rivers.

England had known relative peace for twelve years; but a royal minority threatened to unleash all the tensions created by Edward's patronage of the Woodville family and inflamed by Clarence's execution. On his deathbed Edward had foreseen the worst, and striven to prevent it. He entrusted his son not to the Queen but to his brother Richard, who was named Protector. Richard could command the obedience of older nobility who despised the Queen and the swarm of relatives whom the king had endowed with high office, titled husbands and wealthy heiresses. As a further insurance he persuaded two particular rivals, Lord Hastings and the Queen's eldest son by her first marriage, Thomas Grey, Marquess of Dorset, to shake hands in a formal gesture of reconciliation.

But these hatreds were more than skin deep. While preparations were still in hand for Edward's lavish funeral, the Queen's party took action to protect themselves against the reprisals they considered inevitable if the king's will were allowed to take effect. Their principal asset was time. Until Richard and the rest of the peers of the realm reached London, they commanded a slender majority in the Council. Besides her son Dorset and her two brothers Lionel and Edward, the Queen could count on the support of two important clerics – Thomas Rotherham, Chancellor and Archbishop of York, and John Morton, Bishop of Ely. With these allies, the Woodvilles passed a resolution that Richard's protectorship should be replaced by a Regency Council headed, but not dominated, by the Duke of Gloucester. 'By this means', Mancini later reported with the benefit of hindsight, 'the Duke would be given due honour and the royal authority greater security.... If the government were committed to one man he might easily usurp the sovereignty.' Mancini also reminds us of the Woodvilles' motives when he adds that 'all who favoured the Queen's family voted for this proposal, as they were afraid that if Richard took the crown, or even governed alone, they who bore the blame of Clarence's death would suffer death or at least be ejected from their high estate'.

To give legal and military sanction to their *coup* the Woodvilles further proposed to bring the young King to Westminster for his coronation as soon as possible with as many armed men as Earl Rivers could summon on the road from Ludlow. Under the dire precedent of Henry VI's reign, Edward's minority would end with his crowning and the boy would be free to choose his own advisers. But the thought of Edward arriving with a Woodville army at his back alarmed even the Queen's supporters. The majority bowed to Lord Hastings's threat to retire like Warwick to Calais, of which he was Governor. The size of Edward's escort was fixed at 2,000 men.

Richard was kept fully informed of these developments by couriers from Lord Hastings, who urged the Protector to put himself at the head of an army and race to London before Rivers arrived from Ludlow. But Richard was unwilling to risk a head-on collision with the Woodvilles. For the moment he contented himself with a polite but firm letter to the Council, stressing his devotion to his nephews and warning them not to enact anything contrary to his brother's will.

He then proceeded to York, according to the Croyland Chronicler, 'with a becoming retinue, each person being arrayed in mourning'. Here, 'he performed a solemn funeral service for the king, the same being accompanied with plenteous tears. Constraining all the nobility of these parts to take the oath of fealty to the late King's son, he himself was the first to take the oath.' Richard's letter made a favourable impression in London, and won over a number of waverers to his cause. Nevertheless the Council fixed the coronation date for 4 May, and instructed Rivers to make sure that the king arrived not later than 1 May. Overriding all objections with calculated arrogance, the Marquess of Dorset is said to have told

Lord Hastings and his supporters, 'We are so important that even without the king's uncle we can make and enforce these decisions.'

Shortly after Edward IV had been laid to rest in St George's Chapel at Windsor on 20 April, Richard left York for Northampton with a retinue of about six hundred men. At Northampton he was to join Rivers and the king for the final stage of their progress to London. Clearly neither party expected violence from the other, since Richard arrived with a retinue he knew to be outnumbered, and Rivers was under no compulsion to consent to the meeting in the first place. When Richard arrived on 29 April, as arranged, he learned that the king's escort had already passed through the town and were now quartered twelve miles closer to London at Stony Stratford. Shortly before supper Earl Rivers rode back to Northampton with a small following and presented Edward's greetings to his uncle. He explained the king's removal to Stony Stratford by pointing out that Northampton was too small for both their retinues. Richard politely invited the Earl to stay to supper. They could ride together to join the king in the morning.

During the meal Richard received a second visitor in the person of Henry Stafford, Duke of Buckingham. 'Harre Bokingham', as he signed himself, was the joker in the royal pack who played out the tragedy of Richard III. Lineal descendant of Thomas of Woodstock, Duke of

St George's Chapel, Windsor

The magnificent perpendicular Chapel dedicated to St George in Windsor Castle was begun by Edward IV, and work progressed constantly up to Richard III's death. On Edward's death in April 1483, his body was taken first to Westminster Abbey for the funeral service. It was then buried at Windsor. Richard erected a two-storeyed chantry chapel to his brother in the north choir aisle. The chapel remains very much a monument to Edward, as it is full of his personal badges on the stonework and carved in wood.

Frieze of angels with sunbursts – the symbol of Edward IV – in their crowns and in the stonework below. This forms part of the Rutland Chantry set up in memory of the eldest sister of Edward IV and Richard III, Anne, Duchess of Exeter.

Roof boss from the north choir aisle, showing Edward IV and Bishop Beauchamp, Master of the Works at Windsor, kneeling before the Cross of Gneth, a palladium seized from the Welsh by Edward III during his campaigns, and originally housed in the Chapel.

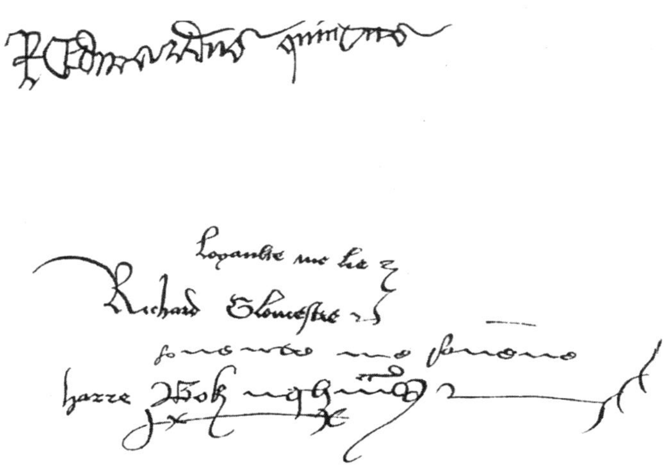

A piece of parchment bearing at the top the signature Edwardus Quintus, with below Richard's motto, Loyaulte me lie, and his signature; and at the bottom Souvente me souvene and 'Harre Bokingham', the motto and signature of Buckingham. This was probably written at St Albans, on 3 May, when the young King halted overnight with Richard and Buckingham on their journey to London.

Gloucester, fifth son of Edward III, he ranked as the first peer of England after Richard and the king's nine-year-old brother Richard, Duke of York.

He also harboured a deep-seated grudge against the Queen, for, after his father was killed fighting for the House of Lancaster in 1455, he became a royal ward and was saddled with a Woodville wife. Ever anxious to feather the family nest, Queen Elizabeth had bestowed on him the hand of her younger sister Catherine 'whom', according to Mancini, 'he scorned to wed on account of her humble origins'. No doubt he saw in Richard the instrument of his revenge.

When Rivers and his companions had retired to bed, Buckingham, Richard and their advisers settled down to a midnight conference. Clearly they had met at Northampton by design: but it is doubtful whether they could have arranged in advance the plan that was now proposed for the following morning. Buckingham's later career will show that he was ambitious, conceited and reckless. He was also an accomplished and persuasive speaker. He must now have pointed out to Richard the danger of pursuing the prudent course he had so far undertaken. Once Rivers had delivered the king to his mother in London and set a crown on his head, only a civil war could unseat the Woodvilles. They were outnumbered – even with the 300 men that Buckingham had brought from London – but in London the odds would be even longer. If they were to act, it must be now.

At dawn on 30 April Richard ordered the arrest of Rivers, and posted guards on the road to prevent the news from reaching Stony Stratford. Accompanied by a troop of soldiers, the two Dukes galloped the twelve miles to Stratford and requested an audience with the king. The interview was brief and rather stilted. Richard began by offering his condolences on the death of the king's father, which he blamed on his ministers and their encouragement of his vices. The same men were guilty of conspiring to ambush the Protector on the road to

London. Edward objected that he had every confidence in his father's ministers and intended to entrust the government to the peers of the realm and the Queen, upon which Buckingham broke in to say that women had no business in the government of a kingdom. If Mancini's account is to be believed, Edward must have been a precocious child and well-rehearsed in his role – an important point in the light of later events. Nevertheless, the interview ended, in Thomas More's account, with the king in tears. His half-brother Lord Richard Grey and his Chamberlain, Sir Thomas Vaughan, were placed under arrest. The king's Welsh escort, with no word from its leaders, was told to go home, and the Dukes returned to Northampton with their captives.

The news reached London at midnight and sent the Queen scurrying with her remaining children to take sanctuary in Westminster Abbey. By the morning of 1 May the city was in uproar. The Marquess of Dorset tried to raise an army to recapture the king, but gave up to join the Queen in sanctuary when he saw that public opinion sided with the Protector. The Thames was swarming with boatloads of Richard's supporters who had come out to cut the Queen's communications with the city. Archbishop Rotherham of York, who had rashly delivered the Chancellor's seal to the Queen, now sent a messenger to reclaim it. Lord Hastings did his best to lower the political temperature by calling a meeting of the remaining lords at St Paul's and explaining, in Thomas

More's words, that 'the Duke of Gloucester was sure and fastly faithful to his prince and that the Lord Rivers and Lord Richard [Grey] were, for matters attempted by them against the Dukes of Gloucester and Buckingham, put under arrest for their surety, not for the king's jeopardy'. The city authorities were also soothed by a letter from Richard, promising an early date for the coronation.

The king and the two Dukes made their entry into London on 4 May. As proof of the villainy of the Queen's family, the procession was headed by four horse-drawn cartloads of weapons embellished with the Woodville insignia, and a group of street-criers who proclaimed that these arms had been placed in secret *caches* on the city outskirts. This gambit rather backfired since a number of the onlookers knew that the armouries had been established by Edward IV for use against the Scots. The procession made its way to the Bishop of London's Palace at St Paul's, where the king was safely lodged. On the same day the Lords, Bishops, Mayor and Aldermen were invited to take the oath of allegiance.

For the moment the future seemed secure. The non-aligned members of the Council, whose prime concern was not to side with Richard or the Queen but to prevent an outbreak of violence, were relieved to find that the transfer of power had been achieved without bloodshed. 'With the consent and goodwill of all the Lords', the Croyland Chonicle reports, 'the Duke of Gloucester was invested with power to order and forbid in every matter, just like another king.' The coronation was now to take place on 24 June, and on the following day the Lords and Commons assembled in Parliament would be asked to ratify the protectorate. At Buckingham's suggestion the king was moved to the more spacious royal apartments in the Tower.

Richard was happy to leave the membership of the Council virtually unchanged. Even Rotherham kept his seat, although his indiscretion with the seal lost him the chancellorship. The new Chancellor was John Russell, Bishop of Lincoln – an appointment that earned the approval even of Richard's enemies. If the absence of Woodvilles left a vacuum, it was filled by the Duke of Buckingham who was also rewarded with wide grants of authority in Wales and the West Country.

The Woodvilles were not forgotten. One member of the family – Sir Edward Woodville – was still at large in the Channel with a fleet that had sailed on 29 April to clear the seas of French and Breton pirates. To persuade the sailors to return to port, Richard offered a free pardon to all but the leaders. Thanks to the ingenuity of two Genoese sea-captains who persuaded Sir Edward's men to drink themselves insensible and then tied them up, the ruse was successful. Sir Edward himself managed to escape to Brittany with only two ships.

Although Rivers, Grey and Vaughan were safely in custody in Richard's northern strongholds, the Protector felt the need to justify his actions at Stony Stratford by bringing charges of treason against them. In this instance the bishops – civil servants who formed the backbone of the neutral peace party in the Council – overrode him. Clearly the tale of the intended ambush cut little ice in government circles. The Council were also keen to reach some arrangement with the Queen who was still cooped up in sanctuary. If she could be persuaded to come out with her children and accept an honourable retirement as Queen Dowager, all rifts would be healed. Negotiations dragged on until the first week in June, but Elizabeth made no move, reluctant either to accept defeat or to trust her brother-in-law's assurances.

Shortly after 5 June, when Anne arrived from Middleham to join her husband, a new crisis erupted suddenly. On 10 and 11 June Richard fired off a series of letters to his friends and supporters in the North. 'We heartily pray you', he wrote to the Corporation of York, 'to come unto us to London in all the diligence ye can possible... with as many as ye can make defensibly arrayed, there to aid and assist us against the Queen, her bloody adherents and affinity, which have intended and daily doth intend to murder and utterly destroy us and our cousin the Duke of Buckingham and the royal blood of this realm.'

The urgency of the letters makes little sense unless the ranks of the Queen's 'bloody adherents' had been swelled by a new recruit of some importance. This was none other than Lord Hastings. Towards the end of May, apparently, he and Archbishop Rotherham, Lord Stanley and Bishop

Morton had fallen into the habit of holding their own informal meetings in the Tower while Richard's intimates gathered around him at his house of Crosby's Place. The grouping of these four was in itself a danger signal, since it signified a rift between the Protector's personal supporters and the men who had formed the inner circle of Edward IV's advisers. But Richard did not feel unduly threatened until he caught wind of a *rapprochement* between Hastings and the Queen.

What could have persuaded Hastings to turn against the man whose interests he had defended so vigorously in the weeks of crisis following the death of Edward IV? Sir Thomas More and Tudor historians readily persuaded themselves that Hastings bitterly regretted his support when he learned of Richard's intention to usurp the Crown. It was his loyalty to Edward V and the memory of his father that caused Hastings to repent.

This notion cannot be disproved, but it seems unlikely on two counts. Family loyalty is hardly the dominant motif of the Wars of the Roses: uncles, cousins and brothers had been fighting and killing each other since 1455 and traded their allegiance whenever it suited their interests. Hastings had never turned his coat on Edward IV but there is no reason to suppose that he would have risked his life for Edward V and the hated Woodvilles unless loyalty was cemented with self-interest. In the second place, there is no evidence that at this time Richard had made up his mind to disinherit his nephews. The draft of

Chancellor Russell's speech for the opening of Parliament has survived, and it states clearly that the first business of the Parliament was to confirm Richard's title as Protector.

Hastings turned to the Woodvilles in June for precisely the same reason as he turned to Richard in April – because his interests were threatened from another quarter. By upholding Richard's claims during the Protector's absence in the North, he doubtless hoped to be rewarded with the lion's share of the spoils and the most important voice in his Council. However, he soon realised that it was Buckingham who had adopted the role of Kingmaker. Buckingham rode beside Richard when the Protector entered London, and Buckingham was rewarded with almost vice-regal powers in Wales and the West. As Lord Chamberlain to Edward V, Hastings could still hope to recoup his position after the coronation. But here again he was disappointed, when Richard proposed to extend his authority until the king came of age.

The remedy that Richard applied to Hastings's disaffection was drastic and quick. On 13 June he struck, without waiting for his reinforcements from Yorkshire. While the official side of the Council was in session at Westminster, Richard summoned the four offenders, Buckingham, Howard and a number of his personal staff to a meeting at the Tower. What followed is vividly described by Sir Thomas More, who derived his information from one of those present – John Morton, Bishop of Ely. The Protector entered the Council

Chamber at nine o'clock, 'excusing himself that he had been from them so long, saying merely that he had been asleep that day. And after a little talking unto them, he said unto the Bishop of Ely: "My Lord, you have very good strawberries at your garden in Holborn, I require you let us have a mess of them."' Shortly after opening the meeting Richard asked the Councillors to excuse him for a moment and left the room. Between 10 and 11 a.m., 'he returned into the chamber among them, all changed, with a wonderfully sour angry countenance, knitting the brows, frowning and fretting and gnawing on his lips'. The Council sat stunned by this sudden change. Then Richard asked them, '"What were they worthy to have, that compass and imagine the destruction of me, being so near of blood unto the king and Protector of his royal person and realm?"' To this Hastings replied '"that they were worthy to be punished as heinous traitors, whatsoever they were". "That is yonder sorceress, my brother's wife", cried Richard, "and others with her."'

Still unaware of what lay in store for him, Hastings was relieved to hear that Richard had cast those familiar bogeymen, the Woodvilles, as the villains of his little drama. But the alarm was clearly sounded when the Protector went on to accuse Jane Shore of abetting the Queen in her sorcery. For Jane, once Edward's favourite mistress, now shared the Lord Chamberlain's bed. Nevertheless Hastings repeated that any such traitors deserved punishment, if they could be proved guilty.

'"What," exclaimed Richard, "thou servest me, I wean, with ifs and with ands, I tell thee they have so done, and that I will make good on thy body, traitor." And therewith as in a great anger, he clapped his fist upon the board a great rap. At which token given, someone cried "Treason!" without. Therewith a door clapped, and in come there rushing men in harness, as many as the chamber might hold.' Hastings, Stanley, Rotherham and Morton were promptly arrested. A priest was brought so that Hastings could make his peace with God. Minutes later he was 'brought forth into the green beside the Chapel within the Tower, and his head laid down upon a log of timber and there striken off'.

Richard promptly sent for a number of important citizens, dressed himself up in rusty armour and explained to them that his strange attire was due to the discovery that Hastings and others had planned to assassinate himself and Buckingham at the Council table. A proclamation to this effect was immediately published to forestall another panic in the city.

Hastings's execution was characteristic of Richard's response to a crisis. The remedy was impulsive, direct and quick. If More's narrative is at least half-way accurate, it was also badly staged and politically inept. By taking the short cut, without regard for legal forms, and dressing the affair in a cloak of crude melodrama, he can only have undermined the confidence of the great men on whom his political future depended. The Woodvilles could be roughly dealt with because the baronial class were only too glad to be rid of them; but Hastings was one of them, a popular man and important office-holder, and long a close friend of the late King.

With Hastings dead, Richard felt he had little to fear from the other three conspirators. Perhaps as a gesture to quiet the fears of the nobility, Lord Stanley was restored to the Council almost immediately. Rotherham, who had once before given proof of his ineffectiveness as an opponent, was released after a short imprisonment. Only John Morton, an altogether more subtle and dangerous enemy, was to be kept out of circulation under Buckingham's custody in the Welsh stronghold of Brecon Castle.

Hastings's conspiracy now led Richard to make the most important decision of his life. Hastings's death had narrowed the base of his support to a point where not even the office of Protector, extended until Edward V's majority, seemed a sufficient guarantee for the future. To survive, he must rule, and to rule he must be King. Perhaps the decisive factor, after Hastings's removal, was the personality of the young King. Already at Stony Stratford Edward had shown he was capable of standing up to his uncle in defence of his mother and her family. Dominic Mancini gives further evidence of his precocity: 'In word and deed he gave so many proofs of his liberal education, of polite, nay rather scholarly, attainments far beyond his age.' Most remarkable was 'his special knowledge of literature which enabled him to discourse elegantly, to understand fully, and to declaim most excellently from any work, verse or prose, that came into his hands, unless it were from among the more abstruse authors'. With his character and intellect already cast to this degree, Edward could hardly be expected to cherish the man who had imprisoned his favourite uncle, Earl Rivers, sent his mother and brother into sanctuary and now beheaded his Lord Chamberlain not a stone's throw from the royal apartments.

Any doubts that Richard was now committed to obtaining the Crown for himself were dispelled three days later on Monday 16 June when the Council met to discuss the removal of Edward's younger brother, Richard, Duke of York, from the sanctuary of Westminster Abbey to the Tower. The two Dukes, accompanied by the Archbishop of Canterbury, Cardinal Bourchier, and a retinue of armed men, proceeded to Westminster by barge. Richard was prepared to use force if necessary, but in order to avoid a violation of sanctuary the Archbishop went in to persuade the Queen to surrender her son voluntarily. Elizabeth was probably not deceived by Bourchier's promise that the boy would be restored after his brother's coronation, but she bowed to the threat of force. The Protector embraced his nephew affectionately at the door of the Painted Chamber and accompanied him to the Tower.

With the princes in his power and his northern followers expected in London within the week, Richard lacked only a legal fiction to justify his claim to the throne. For this purpose he dredged up the story of Edward's marriage contract with Lady Eleanor Butler – a daughter of Old Talbot, the 'Terror of the French'. If true, this story is another example of Edward's disastrous passion for older women. Lady Eleanor was the widow of Sir Thomas Butler and died in 1468. Had the engagement taken place, it would have invalidated his subsequent marriage to Elizabeth Woodville and made bastards of her children. There is in fact no reason to suppose that the story was not true; Edward could never resist a pretty face and troth plight was a common device for coaxing reluctant virgins into bed. Clarence had cast the same aspersions on Edward's marriage six years before, and Robert Stillington, the Bishop of Bath and Wells, claimed to have acted as Edward's go-between in the affair. The news was broken to the people of London on 22 June in a carefully staged sermon at Paul's Cross. Richard selected as his mouthpiece the Lord Mayor's brother, Dr Ralph Shaa, who took as his text the Old Testament quotation *'Spuria vitulamina non agent radices alias'* – 'Bastard slips shall not take deep root'.

In the meantime, the Lords and Commons, originally summoned in May to ratify Richard's protectorate in Parliament, were beginning to arrive in London. Richard, Buckingham and their agents were kept feverishly busy,

Details from a military roll, painted in 1480 for Sir Thomas Holme, Clarenceux King of Arms. Altogether the arms of 248 knights are depicted, from the counties of Suffolk, Essex and Kent.

sounding out opinions and canvassing for support. Richard exchanged the black cloth of mourning he had worn since his brother's death for an outfit of purple velvet, and paraded through the streets of the capital with an army of retainers. The great hall at Crosby's Place was thronged every day at dinner-time with the Protector's guests. On 24 June the Duke of Buckingham enlarged on the theme of Dr Shaa's sermon with an appeal to the Mayor and leading citizens at the Guildhall. He laid great stress on the abuses of government and the financial exactions that had marked the Woodville ascendancy. Under Richard's rule he offered them, 'the surety of your own bodies, the quiet of your wives and your daughters, the safeguard of your goods; of all which things in times past ye stood evermore in need'. Who had been able to count himself master of his own possessions 'amoung so much pilling and polling, amoung so many taxes and tallages, of which there was never end and often time no need?'. Reiterating Richard's rightful claim to the throne 'which ye well remember substantially declared unto you at Paul's Cross on Sunday', Buckingham reminded them that the title of King was no child's office. 'And that great wise man well perceived when he said: woe is that Realm, that hath a child to their King.' The Duke, according to Sir Thomas More, was 'marvellously well spoken'; and one eye witness was much impressed by the fact that he did not even pause to spit between sentences. Nevertheless, the speech had a cool reception until the Duke's servants, at the back of the Hall, threw their caps into the air with shouts of 'King Richard, King Richard'.

Even if the people of London still had their reservations, the Parliament that met at Westminster on Wednesday 25 June, was not disposed to argue. The majority were probably content with any arrangement that promised an end to civil strife. Others who still nursed private grudges against the Woodvilles gladly assented to a measure that ensured their eclipse. And Richard's opponents were prepared to bide their time, cowed for the moment by Hastings's fate and the presence in the capital of so many northerners. Unanimously, the Parliament assented to a document that followed much the same lines as Buckingham's speech in the Guildhall and was couched in the form of a petition to the Duke of Gloucester to take the Crown. On the following day a deputation, headed by none other than the Duke of Buckingham, made its way to the Protector at Baynard's Castle and presented their petition. In keeping with his taste for amateur dramatics, Richard feigned surprise and reluctance before he acceded to more shouts of 'King Richard, King Richard'. The nobility pressed forward to take the oath of allegiance, and King Richard rode in state to Westminster Hall. Here he laid formal claim to his title by seating himself on the marble chair of King's Bench.

While the Lords and Commons were listening to the petition at Westminster, a more melancholy scene was enacted in Yorkshire. Under the supervision of the Earl of Northumberland and Sir Richard Ratcliffe, Anthony, Earl Rivers, Lord Richard Grey and Sir Thomas Vaughan were executed at Pontefract. Witnesses were surprised to learn that the magnificent and talented Earl wore a hair shirt next to his body. Thus Richard signified his triumph over the Woodvilles by killing the one member of the family whose talents and popularity might have redeemed the greed and cruelty of his kin and threatened the ascendancy of his executioner.

In London arrangements were in hand for the most magnificent coronation of the century. Rich ermines, velvets and cloth-of-gold, so lately intended for Edward V's enthronement, were made to serve the occasion of Richard's. While the Master of the Wardrobe laboured to fulfill his contract, Lord John Howard prevailed on the king to confer on him the dukedom of Norfolk and the right to bear the crown to Westminster Abbey as High Steward of England. At the beginning of July, the king held a review of the 5,000 men of Yorkshire, Northumberland and Westmorland who had at last arrived under the command of the Earl of Northumberland. The review took place at Moor Fields and provoked some disparaging comments from Londoners who noted their rusty gear and bedraggled appearance.

On 6 July 1483, the king and queen, preceded by heralds and trumpeters, walked barefoot in procession to the Abbey. Behind the bishops and Cardinal Bourchier came Northumberland with the Sword of Mercy, Lord

Stanley with the Constable's mace, Richard's brother-in-law John de la Pole, Duke of Suffolk with the sceptre and Suffolk's eldest son John, Earl of Lincoln with the orb. These were followed by the newly-created Duke of Norfolk who carried the crown, and his son, Thomas Howard, Earl of Surrey, with the Sword of State. The king himself was flanked by Viscount Lovell and the Earl of Kent bearing the Swords of Justice. Buckingham held Richard's train, and behind him walked the remaining earls and barons of the realm. After the king's procession came the Queen's, her regalia borne by two earls and a viscount. At the high altar Richard and Anne stripped to the waist and were anointed with the chrism. They then changed into cloth-of-gold and Cardinal Bourchier set the crowns on their heads. A *Te Deum* was sung and the royal couple received communion, before they returned to the dais at Westminster Hall for the coronation banquet.

For King Richard III the coronation was a triumph. Not only had it set a new precedent in splendour, but it had also been attended by virtually the entire peerage of England, including Henry Tudor's mother, Margaret Beaufort, Countess of Richmond, who had carried Anne's train, and the Queen Dowager's brother-in-law, Viscount Lisle. And all this had been achieved at the cost of only four lives.

Looking back over the crowded months of April, May and June 1483, it is easy to see how the Tudor historians, reading history backwards, came to the conclusion that

Richard's path to the throne was carefully planned from the moment he left York. The clockwork sequence of events from the seizing of Edward V, the execution of Hastings, the abduction of the Duke of York, Dr Shaa's sermon, to the mummery of the petition – hint at a cold-blooded and cynical intelligence systematically removing the obstacles that lay between Richard and the inheritance of his nephew. Even Dominic Mancini, who wrote his account only six months later and drew no pension from the Tudors, saw Richard's usurpation in this light.

Yet this portrait is too glib to be convincing. It does not mesh with what is known of Richard in previous years – the years of service as a soldier and an administrator with a distaste for courtly intrigues and political in-fighting. The portrait makes better sense if Richard is seen as a man whose eyes were only by degrees opened to the logical consequences of his own actions. His reaction to each succeeding crisis bears the mark of an impulsive man of action taking the short cut to his immediate objective without pausing to work out the long-term effects. If Richard is to be judged, then he must be accused not of too much guile, but of too little.

5

'The Most Untrue Creature Living'

August–November 1483

Lord Hastings dead, the Queen Dowager in sanctuary, the boy King in the Tower, the capital invaded by wild northerners, the Duke of Gloucester King. . . News travelled slowly in fifteenth-century England, and the revolutionary events of the past two months had set the whole country buzzing with wild rumours and unsubstantiated gossip. The new King needed to therefore show himself to his subjects, dispense justice and favours with an open hand, and promise to be every man's good lord. Two weeks after his coronation Richard set out on a royal progress through the West Country and the Midlands to Yorkshire and the North.

But first the three men who had made his usurpation possible received their rewards. Buckingham had the lion's share: he was appointed Constable and Great Chamberlain of England. In addition Richard recognised his long-standing claim to a huge part of the de Bohun inheritance, with an annual income of over £700. To the Earl of Northumberland went the wardenship of the West March and Richard's palatinate in Cumberland. John Howard, the newly-created Duke of Norfolk, received Crown lands worth about £1,000 a year in Suffolk, Essex, Kent and Cambridgeshire. The princely extent of these grants, which virtually created three principalities in Wales and the West Country, in the North, and in East Anglia, show how desperately narrow had become the clique on which Richard's power rested.

Genealogy from a roll of the reign of Edward IV, showing the descent of the rival Houses of Lancaster and York from Edward III.

The Battle of Barnet, fought on 14 April 1471 between the forces of Edward IV and those of his cousin, Warwick the Kingmaker. Richard, Duke of Gloucester commanded the King's van in his first major battle. The illustration is taken from a condensed version of a contemporary chronicle known as the *Historie of the Arrivall of Edward IV*.

(*Left*) Edward IV, portrait by an unknown artist.

(*Below*) Anthony Woodville, Earl Rivers, presenting the *Dictes and Saying of the Philosophers* to his brother-in-law, Edward IV. This was one of the first books printed by William Caxton at his press near Westminster Abbey. Elizabeth Woodville stands to the far right with Edward Prince of Wales in front.

Stained-glass window from Canterbury Cathedral, portraying the family of Edward IV. Left to right, Richard, Duke of York, Edward, Prince of Wales, Edward IV, Elizabeth Woodville, Princesses Elizabeth, Cecilia, Anne, Catherine and Mary.

Part of the Rous Roll, showing Richard III flanked by his wife Anne Neville, and his son Edward, who died in 1484 at the age of nine.

(*Above*) Anne Neville, younger daughter of the Kingmaker, who was first married to Henry VI's son Edward, and then in 1472 married Richard, Duke of Gloucester.

(*Below*) Richard III, portrait by an unknown artist. This is a sixteenth-century version of the standard portrait of the King, probably taken from life, but now lost. Another, earlier version is in the Royal Collection.

John Howard, 1st Duke of Norfolk, who was killed at Bosworth. The inscription shows the message given to Howard before the battle – 'Jockey of Norfolk be not too bold, For Dickon thy master is bought and sold.'

Elizabeth of York, Edward IV's eldest daughter, who was to marry Henry Tudor. Portrait by an unknown artist.

Ruins of Sheriff Hutton Castle, Yorkshire, one of Richard's principal residences in the North. After the death of his son, Richard created a royal household at Sheriff Hutton for his nephews.

Richard III, by an unknown artist, now in the possession of the Society of Antiquaries. This portrait is the only early variant from the standard portrait.

(*Left*) Henry Tudor, painted when King, by Michel Sittow in 1505.

(*Below*) The plight of the Princes in the Tower captured the imagination of many artists, especially during the Romantic period. Here Paul Delaroche gives his version of their last days in the Bloody Tower.

On about 20 July the royal cortège set out from Windsor. Anxious to impress on his subjects that he ruled not by force but by consent, Richard dispensed with an armed escort and was accompanied instead by a magnificent retinue of the principal officers, lay and clerical, of his kingdom. By 23 July they were at Reading. At Oxford the king was entertained by Magdalen's founder, William Waynflete, Bishop of Winchester, and attended two scholarly debates on moral philosophy and theology. At nearby Woodstock he restored to the inhabitants some lands that Edward had annexed to the forest of Whichwood. To the city of Gloucester he granted a new charter of liberties. The abbot of Tewkesbury, whose abbey housed the bones of Clarence and of Henry VI's son, Prince Edward, received a donation of £300. At Warwick early in August, Richard was joined by his Queen. And so, by way of Coventry, Leicester and Nottingham, the procession came to Pontefract where Richard paused to prepare for the climax of his triumphant progress – the State entry into York and the investiture of his son Edward as Prince of Wales.

The king's secretary, John Kendal, had written in advance to the Mayor, Recorder, Aldermen and Sheriffs of York instructing them 'to receive His Highness and the Queen as laudably as their wisdom can imagine'. The city streets were to be hung 'with cloth of arras, tapestry-work and other; for that there come many southern Lords and men of worship with them which will mark greatly your receiving Their Graces'. On 29 August the Mayor and other local dignitaries duly turned out in scarlet and red gowns to greet their Sovereign outside the city walls. His retinue included six bishops; five earls; Lord Stanley, the Steward of the Household; Viscount Lovell, the Lord Chamberlain; Sir William Hussey, the Chief Justice; Alexander, Duke of Albany; the Spanish Ambassador, de Sasiola; and a great train of royal household officials.

An even more magnificent spectacle took place on Sunday 7 September, after a week of plays, banquets, speeches and pageants. This was the day selected for the ten-year-old Earl of Salisbury's investiture as Prince of Wales. The survival of a letter dated 30 August to the Master of King's Wardrobe, requisitioning large quantities of satins, silks, velvet and cloth-of-gold, suggests that the investiture may have been a last-minute addition to Richard's programme. The order included no less than 13,000 fustian badges emblazoned with his device of the silver boar and 'three coats of arms beaten with fine gold for our own person'. Forty trumpeters heralded the arrival of the royal party at York Minster, where the Prince was invested with a plain gold coronet and a golden rod. In honour of the occasion de Sasiola was knighted and received a collar of gold. It was, as Henry VII's official historian, Polydore Vergil, testified, 'a day of great state for York... there being three princes wearing crowns – the king, the Queen and the Prince of Wales'.

William of Wykeham, Bishop of Winchester, founded a grammar school at Winchester and New College at Oxford, in the late fourteenth century. These drawings are taken from a life of William of Wykeham, produced after 1464. Portrait group with William in the centre, seated, holding a model of New College Chapel.

While Richard was busy impressing his subjects with the majesty of his office, powerful forces were conspiring in the South to deprive him of it. Once the initial shock of the usurpation had worn off, some form of reaction on the part of the dispossessed was only to be expected. Most prominent among the dispossessed were, of course, the Woodvilles. The ex-Queen's relatives – the Marquess of Dorset, Sir Richard Woodville and Lionel Woodville, Bishop of Salisbury – formed the sinews of a plot that bound together the chronic discontent of the Kentishmen, the outrage felt by the old guard of Edward IV's personal friends and retainers, and the traditional outposts of Lancastrian loyalism in the south-west. The Wars of the Roses had a habit of uniting strange bed-fellows in a common aim: to these was now added the alliance of Woodville and Lancaster, created by the pervasive rumour that Edward IV's sons had been quietly murdered in the Tower, or spirited away to some northern fortress whence they would never emerge.

These rumours transformed the prospects of a penniless young exile at the Court of Francis, Duke of Brittany. For Henry Tudor, now in his twenty-seventh year, was the sole surviving heir to the claims of the House of Lancaster. On the side of his mother, Margaret Beaufort, he traced his descent from John of Gaunt's extra-marital liaison with Catherine Swynford. The four children of this union, who took the name of Beaufort, were later declared legitimate through the favour of their half-brother, Henry IV, although barred from the royal succession by Act of Parliament. But Acts of Parliament could be repealed as readily as they were made. On his father's side Henry's lineage was equally distinguished and equally tainted with the bar sinister of bastardy. Edmund Tudor, Earl of Richmond was the son of an obscure Welsh gentleman, Owen Tudor, who had found his way into the bed of Henry V's widow, Queen Catherine. Owen claimed to have married the Queen, but the only proof that was ever forthcoming was the three children she bore him. Henry's double illegitimacy offered him some protection during the early years of Yorkist rule and until 1470 he grew up quietly in the household of the Yorkist Earl of Pembroke, William Herbert. But after the Battle of Tewkesbury in 1471 had put paid to Lancastrian hopes and to the last two legitimate Lancastrian claimants, the fourteen-year-old boy became a valuable dynastic chess piece and was smuggled to Duke Francis's Court in Brittany by his uncle, Jasper Tudor. But with the disaffection of the Woodvilles and the old guard of Edward's supporters, the pawn began to assume the stature of a king.

The chief danger to Richard's régime lay in the possibility of a marriage alliance between Henry and one of Edward IV's daughters. In his absence, Richard's Council had already taken steps to guard against this unwelcome prospect by making sure that Edward's daughters remained cooped up at Westminster. The Croyland Chronicle tells us that 'the noble Church of the monks at Westminster, and all the neighbouring parts, assumed the character of a castle and fortress while men of the greatest austerity were appointed to act as keepers thereof'. But the actual link between the rebels at home and the Lancastrian Court in exile was supplied by a new defector who now ranked as the second man in the kingdom.

The king was at Lincoln on 11 October when he heard the astounding news that Buckingham had joined the other conspirators already identified by his informers. Buckingham's rebellion makes no sense unless it is assumed that his earlier support of Richard's cause was, all along, part of a grand design to clear his own path to the throne. Tudor historians later concocted a variety of fables to account for this breathtaking *volte-face* – a quarrel over the de Bohun lands, remorse over the death of the princes, the pervasive wiles of Buckingham's prisoner Bishop Morton – but only Polydore Vergil plumbs the Duke's motives when he reports the rumour that 'the Duke did the less dissuade King Richard from usurping the kingdom by means of so many mischievous deeds that he afterward, being hated both of God and man, might be expelled from the same, and so himself called by the commons to that dignity'. The scheme was not as hare-brained as its ultimate failure made it appear. For Buckingham bore the unquartered arms of Thomas of

Woodstock, youngest son of Edward III, and his lineage was untainted by the bastardy that blemished Henry Tudor's Beaufort claims. Certainly the Yorkists, who had killed his father at St Albans in 1455 and his grandfather at Northampton in 1460, had no claims on his loyalty. Having used Richard to eliminate the senior branch of the Yorkist line he now planned to use the Lancastrian Tudor to unseat the junior branch. The tale of his repentance would in the meantime reconcile the Woodville rebels to co-operating with the late instrument of their downfall.

John Morton, Bishop of Ely, a prisoner at Brecon Castle since Hastings's execution, put Buckingham in touch with Henry Tudor's mother, Margaret Beaufort, Countess of Richmond, and she in turn contacted her son in Brittany. Other couriers linked the Brecon conspirators with the Woodvilles. By these covert means the substance of a tripartite agreement between Henry, Buckingham and the Woodvilles was hammered out. Buckingham pledged his support to Henry's claims; Henry promised to marry the Queen Dowager's eldest daughter, Elizabeth of York. By the end of September all the rebel groups had co-ordinated their plans for a simultaneous rising on 18 October, and Henry Tudor had secured the Duke of Brittany's financial backing for an invasion by sea. Morton was doubtless astute enough to realise that Buckingham the Kingmaker had himself in mind for the throne rather than Henry Tudor, but that was an issue that could wait on Richard's destruction.

In the event Richard was saved by good intelligence, prompt action and foul weather. With so many different factions involved in the plot, it comes as no surprise that a few stool pigeons came to roost in Richard's camp. Within twenty-four hours of hearing the news, the king had sent out the summonses for a royal army to assemble at Leicester by 21 October. Here is the letter he addressed to the Mayor of York:

> BY THE KING
> Trusty and well-beloved: we greet you well, and let ye wit that the Duke of Buckingham traitorously has turned upon us, contrary to the duty of his allegiance, and entendeth the utter destruction of us, you and all other our true subjects that have taken our part; whose traitorous intent we with God's grace intend briefly to resist and subdue. We desire and pray you in our hearty wise that ye will send unto us as many men defensibly arrayed on horseback as ye may goodly make to our town of Leicester the 21st day of this present month without fail as ye will tender our honour and your own weal, and we will see you so paid for your reward as ye shall hold ye well content. Give further credence to our trusty pursuivant this bearer. Given under our signet at our city of Lincoln the 11th day of October.

By the time that he and Northumberland were

reviewing their troops at Leicester on the 21st, Richard was cheered to hear of the swift measures taken by his lieutenant in the South, the Duke of Norfolk, for the defence of London. Finding their way to the capital blocked by Norfolk's men at Gravesend, the Kent and Surrey rebels led by Sir John and Richard Guildford were compelled to withdraw and await the promised arrival of the Duke of Buckingham.

Thanks to the king's effective early warning system and to an exceptional bout of heavy rains that deluged Wales at this moment, the rebel Duke had sufficient troubles of his own.

> In no drowsy manner [reports the Croyland Chronicle] King Richard contrived that, throughout Wales, as well as in all parts of the marches thereof, armed men should be set in readiness around the said Duke, as soon as ever he had set a foot from his home, to pounce upon all his property; who, accordingly, encouraged by the prospect of the Duke's wealth, which the king had, for that purpose, bestowed upon them were in every way to obstruct his progress. The result was, that, on the side of the castle of Brecknock [Brecon], which looks towards the interior of Wales, Thomas, the son of the late Sir Roger Vaughan, with the aid of his brethren and kinsmen, most carefully watched the whole of the surrounding country; while Humphrey Stafford

> partly destroyed the bridges and passes by which England was entered, and kept the other part closed by means of a strong force set there to guard the same.

Drenched by the rains and harassed by the guerillas, Buckingham's retainers lost heart and melted away as they struggled across the Welsh borders into Herefordshire. At Lord Ferrers's manor of Webley the Duke was abandoned even by Bishop Morton, who fled first to the Fen Country, then to Flanders. Sick with fear, the Duke himself deserted what was left of his following. He disguised himself as a commoner and took refuge in the Shropshire cottage of one of his servants, Ralph Bannaster of Wem. For Master Ralph the chief attraction of his guest lay in the £1,000 reward the king had set on his head, and he promptly betrayed the Duke to the local sheriff.

With London in safe hands and Buckingham washed out, Richard was able to concentrate his entire army on the western rebels – Sir Richard Woodville at Newbury, Bishop Lionel Woodville, Sir John Cheyncy and Walter Hungerford at Salisbury, and Dorset, the Courtenays and Thomas St Leger at Exeter – whose only hope now lay in Henry Tudor's fleet. But Henry did not even set out until 31 October, and as Richard's army marched south into Wiltshire, the rebels scattered into sanctuary or sought shelter abroad. When the king entered Salisbury unopposed on 28 October, the great rebellion was over. Buckingham, tried and sentenced by the Vice-Constable, Sir Ralph Assheton, was beheaded in Salisbury market place on Sunday 2 November.

At Exeter on 8 November Richard at last had news of Tudor's ships. Sailing from the Breton port of Paimpol on 31 October with fifteen ships and 5,000 men, the fleet had been scattered at sea by a storm. When he hove to outside Poole Harbour in Dorset with his two remaining ships, the shore was lined with armed men. They were Buckingham's men, they shouted, come to escort him to the Duke. Henry was undeceived. Sailing on to Plymouth he learned that the whole of the West Country lay in Richard's power, and hoisted sail for the return voyage to Brittany.

* * *

One great question still overshadows the episode of Buckingham's rebellion. What *had* happened to the late King's children, Edward and Richard, the princes in the Tower?

The few surviving scraps of contemporary evidence offer only rumour and hearsay. Dominic Mancini unfortunately left England early in July 1483, shortly after Richard's coronation, and does not even mention Buckingham's revolt. Of the prince he tells us only that, after Hastings's execution,

> ...he [Edward] and his brother were withdrawn into the inner apartments of the Tower proper, and day by day began to be seen more rarely behind the bars and windows, till at length they ceased to appear altogether. A Strasbourg doctor, the last of his attendants whose services the king enjoyed, reported that the young King, like a victim prepared for sacrifice, sought remission of his sins by daily confession and penance, because he believed that death was facing him.

Mancini goes on to say that 'already there was a suspicion he had been done away with. Whether, however, he has been done away with, and by what manner of death, so far I have not at all discovered.'

The other contemporary English source – the Croyland Chronicle – confirms that these rumours, reported by Mancini as early as July, were also current on the eve of Buckingham's rebellion in September. 'A rumour', it states, 'was spread that the sons of King Edward had died a violent death, but it was uncertain how.' However, the wording here implies that the rumour may well have been spread by the rebels with malice aforethought.

The only outright accusation of murder that dates from this time appears in a speech made before the Estates General by the French Chancellor at Tours in January 1484. The Chancellor invited the assembled delegates to spare a thought for the children of Edward IV 'whose

The Bloody Tower, known in the fifteenth century as the Garden Tower, because it stood next to the Constable's Garden. It is believed that Richard lodged his young nephews in this tower, and that they were murdered in the bedchamber.

massacre went unpunished, while the assassin was crowned by popular assent'. But the French, who had only a few months before torn up the Treaty of Picquigny, were obviously eager to clutch at any straw that would promote the civil discords of their enemies, and this 'evidence' must be taken with a pinch of salt. De Rochford most probably heard the rumours from Mancini and translated them for propaganda purposes from suspicion into fact.

Stricter confinement, suspicion and propaganda... that is as far as the literary evidence goes. But the dearth of these contemporary sources contrasts strangely with the long and involved story given by Sir Thomas More in his unfinished fragment *The History of King Richard III*. More's account, written forty years later, had such a decisive influence on subsequent versions that it is worth quoting in full:

> King Richard, after his coronation, taking his way to Gloucester to visit in his new honour the town of which he bare the name of his old, devised as he rode to fulfil that thing which he before had intended. And forasmuch as his mind gave him that, his nephews living, men would not reckon that he could have right to the realm, he thought therefore without delay to rid them, as though the killing of his kinsmen could amend his cause and make him a kindly King. Whereupon he sent one John Green, whom he specially trusted, unto Sir

Robert Brackenbury, constable of the Tower, with a letter and credence also that the same Sir Robert should in any wise put the two children to death. This John Green did his errand unto Brackenbury, kneeling before our Lady in the Tower, who plainly answered that he would never put them to death, to die therefore; with which answer John Green, returning, recounted the same to King Richard at Warwick, yet in his way. Wherewith he took such displeasure and thought that the same night he said unto a secret page of his. 'Ah, whom shall a man trust? Those that I have brought up myself, those that I had weaned would most surely serve me, even those fail me and at my commandment will do nothing for me.'

'Sir,' quoth his page, 'there lieth one on your pallet without, that I dare well say, to do your Grace pleasure, the thing were right hard that he would refuse', meaning by this Sir James Tyrell, which was a man of right goodly personage and for nature's gifts worthy to have served a much better prince, if he had well served God and by grace obtained as much truth and good will as he had strength and wit. The man had an high heart and sore longed upward, not rising yet so fast as he had hoped, being hindered and kept under by the means of Sir Richard Ratcliffe and Sir William Catesby, which longing for no more partners of the prince's favour, and namely not for him whose pride they wist would bear no peer, kept him by secret drifts out of all secret trust. Which thing this page well had marked and known. Wherefore, this occasion offered, of very special friendship he took his time to put him forward and by such wise do him good that all the enemies he had, except the devil, could never have done him so much hurt. For upon this page's words King Richard arose (for this communication had he sitting at the draught [privy], a convenient carpet for such a counsel) and came out into the pallet chamber, on which he found in bed Sir James and Sir Thomas Tyrell, of person like and brethren of blood, but nothing of kin in conditions. Then said the king merrily to them: 'What, Sirs, be ye in bed so soon!' and calling up Sir James, broke to him secretly his mind in this mischievious matter; in which he found him nothing strange. Wherefore, on the morrow, he sent him to Brackenbury with a letter, by which he was commanded to deliver Sir James all the keys of the Tower for one night, to the end he might there accomplish the king's pleasure in such thing as he had given him commandment. After which letter delivered and the keys received, Sir James appointed the night next ensuing to destroy them, devising before and preparing the means. The prince, as soon as the protector left that name and took himself as King, had it showed unto him that he should not reign, but his uncle should have the crown. At which word the prince, sore abashed, began to sigh and said: 'Alas, I would my uncle would let me have my life yet, though I lose my kingdom.' Then he that told him the tale used him with good words and put him in the best comfort he could. But forthwith was the prince and his brother both shut up: and all others removed from them, only one called Black Will or William Slaughter except, set to serve them and see them sure. After which time the prince never tied his points, nor aught wraught of himself, but with that young babe his brother lingered in thought and heaviness till this traitorous death delivered them of that wretchedness. [An examination of the remains generally held to be those of the princes shows that Edward V was suffering from a bone disease of the lower jaw and his state of depression may well have been due to ill health rather than any premonition of his fate.] For Sir James Tyrell devised that they should be murdered in their beds. To the execution whereof, he appointed Miles Forest, one of the four that kept them, a fellow fleshed in murder beforetime. To him he joined one John Dighton, his own horsekeeper, a big broad, square, strong knave. Then, all the others being removed from them, this Miles Forest and John Dighton, about midnight (the silly [innocent] children lying in their beds) came into the chamber and suddenly lapped them up among the clothes, so bewrapped them and entangled them, keeping down by force the feather bed and pillows hard unto their mouths, that within a while, smothered and stifled, their breath failing, they gave up to God their innocent souls into the joys of heaven, leaving to the tormentors their bodies dead in the bed. Which after that the wretches perceived, first by the struggling with the pains of death, and after lying still, to be thoroughly dead: they laid their bodies naked out upon the bed, and fetched Sir James to see them. Which, upon the sight of them, caused those murderers to bury them at the stair foot, meetly deep in the ground, under a great heap of stones.

Then rode Sir James in great haste to King Richard, and showed him all the manner of the murder, who give him great thanks and, as some say, there made him knight. But he allowed not, as I have heard, the burying in so vile a corner, saying he would have them buried in a better place, because they were a King's sons. Lo the honourable courage of a King! Whereupon they say that a priest of Sir Robert Brackenbury took up the bodies again, and secretly entered them in such place, as by the occasion of his death, which only knew it, could never since come to light. Very truth is it and well known, that at such times as Sir James Tyrell was in the Tower, for treason committed against the

> most famous prince King Henry the Seventh, both Dighton and he were examined, and confessed the murder in manner above written, but whither the bodies were removed they could nothing tell. And thus have I learned of them that much knew and little cause had to lie, were these two noble princes, these innocent tender children, born of most royal blood, brought up in great wealth, likely long to live to reign and rule in the realm, by traitorous tyranny taken, deprived of their estate, shortly shut up in prison, and privily slain and murdered their bodies cast God knows where by the cruel ambition of their unnatural uncle and his dispiteous tormentors.

More's account, written in 1513, carries a certain glib conviction, because he claims as his source the confession of the alleged assassin, Sir James Tyrell, who was executed for treason in 1502. But to accept it at its face value raises a number of unanswerable questions: why would Sir James make such a damaging confession? Why did Henry VII never have it taken down in writing and circulated? Why does his official historian, Polydore Vergil, omit all mention of the confession?

The lack of incriminating evidence against Richard and the obvious holes in More's testimony have led to some ingenious theorising about Henry VII as the possible assassin. In the summer of 1486 – one year after Bosworth – Henry VII issued not one but two royal

William Caxton: the First English Printer

Caxton was originally a mercer, spending much of his time in Bruges, the central foreign market of the Anglo-Flemish trade. By 1463 he was Acting Governor of the Merchant Adventurers' Company in the Low Countries. When Margaret of York married Charles the Rash, Caxton entered her household as a commercial adviser.

In 1471 Caxton went to Cologne, and there learned the art of printing. He first set up his press in Bruges, and then in 1476 returned to England and established his press at Westminster. He was patronised by many of Edward IV's leading courtiers, including Anthony Woodville, Earl Rivers, whose work was printed on Caxton's presses.

Prologus

Gret chere made our ost to vs euerychon
And to souper sette he vs anon
He serued vs wyth vytaylle at the beste
Strong was the wyne & wel drynke vs lyste
A semely man our oste was wyth alle
For to be a marchal in a lordes halle
A large man he was wyth eyen stepe
A fayrer burgeys is ther non in chepe
Bold of hys speche and wel was y taught
And of manhood lacked he right nought
Eke therto was he right a mery man
And after souper to pleyen he began
And spak of myrthe among other thynges
Whan that we hadde made our rekenynges
He sayd thus now lordynges treuly
Ye be to me right welcome hertly
For by my trouthe yf I shal not lye
I saw not thys yeer so mery a companye

ABOVE: Woodcut of a blacksmith from Caxton's *Game and Play of the Chess* printed *c.*1483.

LEFT: Page from Caxton's edition of Chaucer's Prologue to *The Canterbury Tales*, which he printed in 1483. This depicts the pilgrims feasting on boar's head.

William Caxton presenting his translation of the popular romance *The Recuyell of the Historyes of Troye*, to his patroness, Margaret of York. He printed the *Recuyell* at Bruges in 1474–5, in partnership with Colard Mansion.

pardons in the name of Sir James Tyrell. Using this fact in conjunction with More's narrative, it has been argued that Tyrell did indeed murder the princes, not at Richard's bidding but at Henry's. Added to this there is Henry's rather puzzling failure to make use of Richard's alleged murder of the princes as a weapon in the propaganda war, either before or after Bosworth. Although it would have made sense to publish the princes' death as a means of strengthening his wife Elizabeth's claims to be Edward IV's heiress, there is only a single, indirect reference to the 'shedding of infants' blood' tucked away in the Act of Attainder that he presented to his Parliament in October 1485. Finally, there is the evidence of Henry's shabby treatment of his mother-in-law, the Dowager Queen Elizabeth Woodville. In February 1487 he abruptly had her stripped of her possessions and shut up in a nunnery. This has been taken as evidence of the fact that the Queen Dowager had learned of Henry's guilt in the disposal of her sons, and had to be locked up to prevent her causing a scandal.

The most effective rebuttal of Henry's guilt lies in the only piece of hard evidence we possess. In 1674 workmen demolishing a staircase outside the White Tower discovered a wooden chest containing the skeletons of two children. From both their location and their approximate ages it was immediately assumed that these were the mortal remains of the murdered Princes, concealed where More indicated they were buried, but not removed for reburial elsewhere as he further stated. In 1933 these skeletons were submitted to a medical examination. From the bone formation and the structure of the teeth it was concluded that the skeletons were those of two children aged about twelve and ten respectively. This tallies with the ages of the two Princes in the early autumn of 1483; if these are the skeletons of the princes, and their ages have been accurately assessed, it can be argued that Henry VII is exonerated from any part in their deaths.

By the same logic, if the princes died in the autumn of 1483, there are only two men who could conceivably have been responsible – Richard and Buckingham. Both had the same motive. While Edward IV's children were alive they would provide a focus for legitimist conspiracies. There were numerous precedents for doing away with embarrassing prisoners of royal blood – from King John's nephew Arthur to King Henry VI – to persuade their gaolers that reasons of State overrode the dictates of private conscience.

On two counts Buckingham makes a more plausible villain than Richard. First, his motive was stronger than the king's. By 6 July Richard had already cleared the hurdle of winning the consent of the people who mattered to his usurpation of the Crown. By the simple device of proclaiming his nephews to be bastards he also had a theoretical justification for his successful *coup*. Although the princes would be an embarrassment, they were no longer an obstacle. But, if Buckingham was aiming to depose Richard in his turn, he would have to enlist the support of men who were loyal to the memory of Edward IV – men who would not subscribe to the theory of his children's bastardy. It was thus essential to make sure the princes were dead before he made his bid – and to put the blame on Richard.

This interpretation would help to explain the agreement that Richard reached with the Queen Dowager in February 1484. In return for a guarantee of her daughters' safety, Elizabeth agreed that they should leave the sanctuary of Westminster Abbey and place themselves in Richard's care. This would seem to be an extraordinarily stupid thing to do if she knew – or even suspected – that Richard had already murdered her two sons.

However, the Buckingham theory is snagged by one fatal flaw. If Buckingham was guilty, Richard could have saved himself a lot of trouble by saying so. 'The most untrue creature living' had a lot of crimes laid at his door, but never the murder of the princes. At the risk of complicating the issue still further, we could go on to ask, why did Richard not avail himself of the opportunity to accuse Buckingham, even if he was guilty himself? The simplest answer would be that they were still alive when the Woodville daughters emerged from sanctuary and met their death shortly afterwards. This would be within an acceptable margin of error as far as medical evidence on the skeletons is concerned. It would also tally with the statement in the Great Chronicle of London that the rumours of the princes' deaths were current after Easter 1484.

On balance this too is improbable, for there are more powerful reasons to support the conclusion that the princes were already dead when Richard heard the news of Buckingham's treachery. First of all, the marriage between Elizabeth of York and Henry Tudor, which was negotiated in September 1483, would not have gained the Queen Dowager's assent if she still had reasonable hopes of seeing her two boys alive. Second, Richard never made any attempt to quash the rumours circulating in the autumn of 1483 by parading Edward and Richard in public. Finally, there is no mention of any guarantees for their safety in the pact that brought their sisters out of Sanctuary on 1 March 1484.

As the alternative suspects are eliminated and the time-scale of the murders narrows, Richard's defence begins to appear more and more shaky. It is therefore worth taking a second look at the most convincing circumstantial evidence in his favour – the fact that, on 1 March 1484, the Queen Dowager permitted her daughters to leave the sanctuary of Westminster Abbey. Elizabeth Woodville was no fool. The former widow of a Lancastrian knight, she was canny enough to become the wife of a Yorkist king. She was also hardy enough to have given birth to her elder son twelve years before in the same sanctuary. If she knowingly delivered her daughters to the man who had done away with her sons, she must have been prompted by something more than naïvety or claustrophobia.

Sanctuary, she knew, was not an inviolable privilege. After the battle of Tewkesbury in 1471, Edward IV gave orders for the Lancastrian rebels who had taken refuge in the Abbey to be dragged out and executed. If Richard was determined to get her and her daughters out, she had no reason to suppose his scruples would be any stronger than his brother's. This much is hinted in Croyland Chronicle: 'After frequent entreaties *as well as threats* had been used, Queen Elizabeth, being strongly solicited to do so, sent her daughters from the Sanctuary at Westminster to King Richard.' If sanctuary was unsafe, was there any greater certainty that Richard would respect his promise not to harm her daughters? The wording of his oath provides the clue:

> Memorandum that I, Richard... in the presence of my Lords spiritual and temporal, of you, Mayor and Aldermen of my City of London, promise and swear *verbo regio* and upon these Holy Evangiles of God by me personally touched, that if the daughters of Dame Elizabeth Grey, late calling herself Queen of England, that is to wit Elizabeth, Cecily, Anne, Katherine and Bridget, will come out into me of the Sanctuary of Westminster, and be guided, ruled and demeaned after me, I shall see that they be in surety of their lives, and also do not suffer any

> manner of hurt... in their body and persons by way of ravishment or defouling contrary to their wills....

The terms are what we might expect: it is the witnesses who are the key. Richard's private word of honour was reinforced by a public undertaking, witnessed by Lords, Bishops, Mayor and Aldermen. If the king broke his oath, the whole kingdom would know of it. Every public act that Richard undertook in 1483 – the heralds announcing the discovery of the Woodville arms caches, the staging of Dr Shaa's sermon, the royal progress of July and August, the magnificent investiture of the Prince of Wales – witnesses how sensitive he was to public opinion. The princes might be done away with in secret, but their five sisters would find no safer refuge than in the limelight of Richard's Court.

We have thus come in a full circle back to Richard as the prime suspect and the early autumn of 1483 as the most likely date. The evidence is not conclusive in a legal sense, and never will be. Richard stands convicted not so much by the evidence against him as by the lack of evidence against anybody else.

The murders leave an ineradicable stain on Richard's character. Despite the long list of precedents the act was as shocking then as it appears today. But it does not prove that his nature was warped by a vein of deliberate cruelty. His treatment of the vanquished Nevilles and his defence of Clarence show Richard in a kinder light. It is also more than likely that Buckingham egged him on to the murder as persuasively as he propelled him towards the throne.

More important than the moral issue were the political consequences. The murder of the princes has often been described as a Renaissance solution in the manner later prescribed by Macchiavelli. In fact it was a colossal blunder. Nothing else could have prompted the deflated Woodvilles to hitch themselves to Henry Tudor's bandwagon. In October Richard was rescued from the consequences by the storm that scattered Henry's Breton fleet. But the menace remained and would cast its shadow over the brief twilight of Richard's reign. At the cathedral of Rennes on Christmas Day 1483, Henry Tudor swore a solemn oath in the presence of the Lancastrian Court in exile that he would marry Elizabeth of York. It was both a promise and a warning.

6

The King

1483–4

Returning to his capital on 25 November 1483, Richard received a heartening welcome at Kennington from the Mayor and Aldermen in their scarlet robes, and was escorted to Blackfriars by a troop of horsemen clad in violet. He had survived the first real crisis of his reign with surprisingly little effort. His army had been sent home without striking a blow. The overwhelming majority of the gentry, the cities and even the barons had ignored the rebel call to arms, and signified their consent to his usurpation. The storm clouds gathering in Brittany were not allowed to disturb the magnificent Christmas festivities, which prompted Commynes to declare that Richard 'was reigning in greater splendour and authority than any king of England for the last hundred years'. With one London mercer alone he ran up a bill for £1,200.

Richard was not the sort of man to indulge himself for long in the sybaritic pleasures of the Court. Early in the New Year he was back in the saddle, on a progress through Kent. Unlike the ceremonial tour of the previous summer, this was a strictly business-like affair. During the late rebellion Kent had once again lived up to its reputation as the most troublesome shire in his kingdom. A special oath of allegiance was now administered to the men of Kent by commissioners appointed for that purpose, and one of Richard's most trusted household knights, Sir Marmaduke Constable, was installed at Penshurst to put down the evils of livery and maintenance. The royal proclamation that followed on the heels of the oath is interesting because it puts Richard's political philosophy in a nutshell. Any man who found himself 'grieved, oppressed or unlawfully wronged' was invited to 'make a bill of complaint and put it to his highness, for his grace is utterly determined that all his subjects shall live in rest and quiet, and peaceably enjoy their lands, livelihoods and goods, according to the laws of this his land, which they were naturally born to inherit'. It was a clear recognition that a king must earn his subjects' loyalty with firm, effective government and speedy, impartial justice.

The tragedy of Richard III was that he had so little time to put his good intentions into effect. Nevertheless,

The founding charter of the Tallow-Chandler's Company, issued in 1456. The little figure in the initial is the herald who granted the arms to the Company.

at the first and only Parliament of his reign, which opened on 23 January, he made an impressive beginning.

Unlike the tyrant of legend, Richard had a healthy respect for the assembly of Lords and Commons who met together in the Painted Chamber at Westminster to hear the Chancellor's opening address. Parliament was the highest court of the realm, with a special competence in the larger political issues of the succession, the disinheritance of traitors by act of attainder, the imposition of taxes, the overhaul of the machinery of justice and other great issues touching the welfare of the community as a whole. Over the last two centuries, the knights and burgesses who represented the shires and the towns had won many important privileges, including the right to hold their own deliberations in the refectory of Westminster Abbey under a Speaker of their choice, to put forward collective requests of their own devising, known as common petitions, and to make all Parliamentary legislation conditional on their assent. During the troubled years of Henry VI's reign the Commons had shown themselves particularly aggressive, forcing on the king's Council their proposals for the reform of his slipshod finances, and even impeaching Queen Margaret's favourite minister, the Duke of Suffolk. In Edward IV's capable hands the situation was quickly reversed. Far from resisting reform, it was the king's Council that most actively promoted it and entered into a fruitful partnership with the Commons. This was the precedent that Richard determined to follow.

John Russell's opening speech was originally intended for Edward V's first Parliament, but it would serve as well for Richard's. It was an appeal to the Lords to forget their private quarrels and 'each amiably hearken upon the other, so that they might attend to the welfare of the body politic'. A postscript on the Duke of Buckingham – 'a rotten member of the body' – was added, to drive the lesson home. Business began in earnest on the following Monday, when the Commons paid their King the compliment of choosing his personal confidant, William Catesby, as Speaker. Their first priority was the confirmation of Richard's title: the Act reiterated the story of Edward's precontract with Eleanor Butler, accused Elizabeth Woodville of witchcraft and sorcery, and attributed all the subsequent 'destruction of the noble blood of this land' to her 'ungracious pretensed marriage' to the king. Since Edward's children were bastards and Clarence's had been attainted, Richard was king by right of inheritance, as well as by the election of the three estates assembled in Parliament. Prince Edward, his son, was declared heir apparent.

The attainders came next. Ninety-five men had been singled out as the leaders of the rebellion and had their lands confiscated – twenty-eight from Kent and Surrey, fourteen from Berkshire, thirty-three from Wiltshire and eighteen from the Exeter clique. These measures were not unduly harsh: at least a third of the attainders were subsequently revoked and many of those named had already found refuge at Henry's Court in exile. The two women most closely implicated were treated with generosity. The Duchess of Buckingham, *née* Catherine Woodville, received an annuity. The much more deeply implicated Countess of Richmond suffered no further punishment than having to place her lands in the keeping of her husband, Lord Stanley. Without a doubt, she owed her survival to Stanley who, with his unusually sensitive nose for picking the winner, had remained loyally at Richard's side throughout the crisis.

The remainder of the session was devoted to more constructive work. The Commons approved a whole sheaf of government-sponsored statutes aimed at stopping legal loop-holes and sharp practices. One ensured that juries should be properly qualified and free from intimidation. Another provided that bail should be allowed to men arrested on suspicion of felony. A third put a stop to fraudulent property transfers that concealed from the buyer that a part of the property in question had already been sold to somebody else. These were clearly aimed at local dignitaries who used their position to exploit less powerful neighbours, and they show that Richard was not afraid of causing offence among his more influential subjects in the name of better justice.

In drafting these reforms Richard employed the help of some of the most able and learned men in the kingdom, for, apart from his personal confidants, the backbone of Richard's Council were the churchmen who traditionally staffed the upper echelons of the civil service in the Middle Ages. All of them were professionals with years of service under Edward IV to their names. The Chancellor, John Russell, was an experienced diplomat, as was Thomas Langton, Bishop of St David's, whom Richard would shortly send on a mission to the Pope. Thomas Rotherham, Archbishop of York and Robert Stillington, Bishop of Bath and Wells, were both Cambridge academics and former Chancellors. John Alcock, Bishop of Worcester, became the founder of Jesus College, Cambridge. John Gunthorp, Dean of Wells, was Keeper of the Privy Seal and the royal chaplain, Edmund Chatterton, held a key financial post as Treasurer of the Chamber. These men not only brought a wealth of experience to the Council table, but also provided the vital element of continuity with the previous régime.

If the Commons were impressed by Richard's conscientious programme of legal reforms, they were probably even more gratified by his failure to ask for a Parliamentary subsidy. The military expenses of the previous autumn had proved a heavy drain on his resources and the substantial treasure hoard bequeathed to him by Edward IV was almost depleted. Furthermore, he knew that Henry Tudor would soon try his luck again. To meet the threat more troops would have to be paid, ships fitted out, battlements repaired and garrisons provisioned. His reticence in asking the Commons for money must therefore have been a political gesture. Unless some grandiose chauvinistic venture like the conquest of France was in the offing, the increasingly prosperous middle classes were particularly resentful of direct taxation, and expected the king to maintain his household and meet the day-to-day expenses of government from his own resources. In his earnest effort to win their approval Richard went one step further: he renounced in advance the fund-raising device of voluntary loans or benevolences that had caused so much unfavourable comment during his brother's reign. On 20 February, the last day of Parliament's sitting, the Commons granted him in return the customs revenues, known as tonnage and poundage.

Richard's greatest source of power and wealth lay, in fact, in the Crown lands. At his accession in 1483, these included not only the combined possessions of the Lancastrian and Yorkist kings, but also vast forfeitures of dead or attainted Lancastrian magnates, which Edward had granted to Clarence and to Richard himself, as Duke of Gloucester. This accumulation of manors, castles and townships yielded an annual revenue of nearly £25,000. Even after the salaries of a small army of royal officials had been paid, estate management could be made to show a handsome profit and more than covered the £11,000 needed to support Richard's perambulatory household. For the organisation that administered the Crown lands Richard was again indebted to his profit-conscious brother. Edward IV had been very professional about estate management, appointing men with legal training rather than local squires or knights as his stewards and surveyors, conducting regular audits, and controlling the whole operation through the Treasurer and clerks of his Chamber.

As a usurper Richard was inevitably committed to handing out a fair chunk of his estates as rewards for his supporters. At the time of his coronation a golden shower of grants fell on the not unexpectant trinity of Norfolk, Buckingham and Northumberland. But these grants were only a curtain raiser for those that followed at the end of the year. The confiscations and attainders visited on the rebels of Buckingham's rebellion gave Richard the opportunity to create a whole class of men with a vested interest in his political survival. Buckingham himself was the greatest landowner in England after the king, and the annual value of the lands Richard bestowed on his loyal followers totalled £12,000. It was this redistribution of property – the greatest since Richard II despoiled his opponents in 1398 – that prompted Sir Thomas More's acid comment: 'with large gifts he got him unsteadfast friendship, for which he was fain to pillage and spoil in other places, and got him steadfast hatred'.

The list of recipients again contains the names of the small nucleus of barons who were neither dead nor exiled. Northumberland was granted the extensive holdings of his mother's family, the Poynings, in Surrey, Sussex and the West Country. Lord Stanley and his brother, Sir William, shared in the spoils of Buckingham's Welsh holdings. Other rewards were parcelled out to Norfolk and his son, Thomas Howard, Earl of Surrey, to Richard's nephew, John de la Pole, Earl of Lincoln, and to William Herbert, Earl of Huntingdon, who had married the king's bastard daughter, Catherine. But the largest group were men with a more direct stake in Richard's future, his personal following of knights and esquires, whose rewards were coupled with responsibilities as sheriffs, keepers of castles or guardians of the royal estates. The harsh lessons of the careers of Warwick and Montagu, Clarence and Buckingham had taught Richard not to build his fortunes solely on the shifting sands of baronial loyalty.

The king's preference for men of middle rank, especially for the associates of his lieutenancy in the North, did not pass without comment. The Croyland Chronicler reported that 'the immense estates and patrimonies' collected by attainder were all 'distributed among his northern adherents whom he planted in every spot throughout his dominions, to the disgrace and lasting and loudly expressed sorrow of all the people in the south'.

Of Richard's three closest advisers, two – Francis, Viscount Lovell and Sir Richard Ratcliffe – were former members of his Council in the North. The third, William Catesby, came from the Midlands and was a comparatively recent discovery. This trio was commemorated in the famous rhyme nailed to the door of St Paul's later that year in July:

'The Cat, the Rat and Lovell our dog
Rulen all England under an Hog.'

The king's secretary, John Kendal, had previously served as the Duke of Gloucester's secretary, and was rewarded with the lucrative office of Controller of the Mint. Lord Scrope of Bolton, another of Richard's Northern Council, also belonged to the inner circle of the king's Council. Further down the scale were a number of other northern knights, including James Tyrell; Robert Brackenbury, the Constable of the Tower and Sheriff of Kent; Robert Percy, the king's boyhood friend and Controller of the Household; and Ralph Assheton, the Vice-Constable of England. Richard's trust in these northerners was not misplaced: with one exception all of them would ride with him to Bosworth.

As soon as Parliament had concluded its business Richard was chafing to resume his travels. Two final precautions – both of them reminders that he still had powerful enemies – detained him until the first week of March 1484. One was the agreement negotiated for the release of the Queen Dowager's daughters from sanctuary. The other was a solemn ceremony described by the Croyland Chronicler:

> Shortly after mid-day nearly all the lords of the realm, both spiritual and temporal, together with the higher knights and esquires of the king's household,

> met together at the special command of the king in a certain lower room near the passage which leads to the Queen's apartments; and here each subscribed his name to a kind of new oath... of adherence to Edward, the king's only son, as their supreme lord, in case anything should happen to his father.

Then he was away, with Queen Anne at his side, heading for the cloisters of Cambridge University, and what was to be the last interlude of peace in his short, unhappy reign. During the week they spent at Cambridge, Richard and Anne made generous endowments to King's and Queens' Colleges, which the University promised to remember in a special Mass to be celebrated on 2 May. As the royal cortège left Cambridge, Richard's thoughts turned to the challenges that the new campaigning season would bring: French and Breton ships were preying on English merchantmen; the Scots were stirring on his northern borders; and in Brittany Henry Tudor was gathering his resources for a fresh invasion. On 20 March Richard established his military headquarters behind the massive battlements of Nottingham Castle. Here, poised at the heart of the kingdom, he would be ready to strike wherever danger threatened.

Here too, in the middle of April, he received the news that must have affected him more deeply than any of the bereavements and betrayals that already crowded his life. Edward, Prince of Wales, was dead. A note of emotion is visible even in the terse report of the Croyland Chronicle: 'this only son of his, in whom all the hopes of the royal succession, fortified with so many oaths, were centred, was seized with an illness of but short duration and died at Middleham Castle in the year of our Lord, 1484.... You might have seen his father and mother in a state almost bordering on madness, by reason of their sudden grief.'

The public impact went further than the private grief. Throughout the Wars of the Roses the uncertainty of the succession was at the root of the conflict and invited the aristocracy to further mischief in their own interests. Prince Edward's death now invited the surviving magnates – Norfolk, the Stanleys and Northumberland – to reconsider their allegiance to Richard. Equally important was the psychological effect on the gentry, the merchants and the yeoman classes – men whose tacit consent was vital in turning a successful *coup d' état* into enduring government. They might well reflect that the little known Lancastrian claimant, allied to a Yorkist bride, was better placed to outlaw faction at home and piracy at sea than a childless usurper.

As the war of nerves mounted in the spring and summer, Richard pondered on the choice of his successor. Queen Anne, barren for ten years since Edward's birth, could bear him no more children. The king inclined at first to Clarence's son, Edward, Earl of Warwick. This ten-year-old boy was eventually passed over, not so much because he was Clarence's son but because he was too young and showed signs of being mentally retarded. Edward of Warwick is one of the most pitiable victims of dynastic politics: kept in solitary confinement from the age of five he grew up, according to one report, unable to 'tell a goose from a capon'. Richard did something to alleviate his condition by establishing him with a household in the oak-lined park of Sheriff Hutton, but under Henry VII he was returned to the Tower and eked out his imprisonment until he was executed on a fabricated charge of treason.

Richard's final choice fell on John de la Pole, Earl of Lincoln, eldest son of the Duke of Suffolk and Richard's sister Elizabeth. The young Earl of Warwick was too risky a candidate at this time of crisis, while Lincoln was a grown man, already identified with Richard's government. On 21 August Richard followed Yorkist tradition by appointing the heir apparent Lord Lieutenant of Ireland.

In the meantime Richard laboured to put his kingdom in readiness for war. On 1 May he sent commissions of array to his chief lieutenants, empowering them to call men to his standards at short notice. A network of couriers was set up to link him with his Chancellor's Council in London and with his sentinels on the coasts. However, Richard was not content to wait for Henry to come to him: he was also engaged in organising a diplomatic *coup* whose success would render his military preparations unnecessary.

Relations with Brittany had been fouled from the

start by Duke Francis's attempt to blackmail Richard. In exchange for keeping his guest Henry Tudor on a tight leash, Francis demanded 4,000 English archers to help him in his quarrels with the king of France. Richard refused. Francis responded with generous loans to the Lancastrian exiles and loosed his Breton corsairs on English merchantmen. A vigorous naval campaign undertaken in the winter of 1483–4 led to the conclusion of a truce in April 1484. Since Francis was suffering from some form of mental illness, the government of the duchy was by now in the hands of his more amenable treasurer, Pierre Landois, and when the truce was ratified at Pontefract on 8 June, it contained an additional secret clause. Richard would supply the Bretons with 1,000 archers, provided that the self-styled Earl of Richmond was kept in custody. This accord was apparently followed by further overtures, during which Landois was offered the revenues of the earldom of Richmond if he would deliver Henry Tudor to Richard's agents. Rumours of these proposals came to the attentive ears of John Morton in Flanders. He promptly despatched a warning message to Henry at Vannes. The messenger – a priest named Christopher Urswick – was instructed to continue his journey to the French Court and ask for political asylum on behalf of the Earl of Richmond and his followers. Permission was eagerly granted. The French were in some disarray since the recent death of Louis XI: but Charles VIII's Council were agreed that King Richard was no friend of France. Had he not led the hard-liners who spoke out against the Treaty of Picquigny in 1475, and given fresh proof of his enmity by seeking an alliance with Brittany?

Richmond's next problem was to elude the vigilance of Landois's men and slip over the duchy's borders into France. With only five followers he rode out of Vannes under the pretext of visiting a neighbour. As soon as he was clear of the town, he exchanged clothes with a servant and rode hell for leather towards the frontier. As he crossed into Anjou, those whom Landois sent in pursuit were only an hour's ride behind him.

It was a near miss. But the restless summer brought other achievements to set against this diplomatic failure. Richard's punishing itinerary bears witness to the energy with which he tackled the perennial problems of the Scottish border and the administration of the northern counties. Early in May he visited York, Middleham and Durham. Naval preparations kept him at Scarborough until the second week of June, when he received the Breton embassy at Pontefract. By mid-June he was in York, then on to Scarborough again, and back to York late in July. Haunted by the spectre of Henry Tudor's invasion, Richard was determined to step up the military and diplomatic pressures on the Scots until James III came to his senses and sought a permanent peace. Details of the campaigns he set in motion have not survived, but the Croyland Chronicle reports that the Scots 'sustained a great defeat from our people by land' followed by an equally significant naval victory for the Scarborough squadron. These measures achieved precisely the effect Richard had in mind, for in July James III sent Lord Lisle to open negotiations. Once he had assured himself that the Scots were in earnest, the king gave safe conducts for a formal embassy to attend on him at Nottingham in September.

Equally important was the form of government that Richard established for the North at York on 21 July. A formal Council, under the lieutenancy of the Earl of Lincoln, was to supervise the keeping of the king's peace throughout the counties of Yorkshire, Westmorland and Cumberland. Although Lincoln was appointed Lieutenant in the North, the Council derived its authority from the king, and the household he maintained at Sheriff Hutton was designated the king's household in the North. The detailed instructions Richard dictated for his Council's operation emphasised that 'all letters and writings... be made in our name, and the names to be endorsed with the hand of our nephew of Lincoln below with the words *"per consilium regis"*'.

In effect the Council served as a junior branch of Richard's Council at Westminster. It was to meet every quarter at York to 'hear, examine and order all bills and complaints and other there before them to be served', and was vested with complete authority to cope with public disorder. The military duty of defending the border lay outside its functions and was retained by the Warden General. The Councillors included both local magnates and professional lawyers. Few of their names are known to us. Northumberland, certainly, was a member of the Council, as was Lincoln's brother-in-law, Lord Morley. The retarded Earl of Warwick, who was entrusted to Lincoln's care at Sheriff Hutton, was given a nominal role by merit of his royal blood. Richard's innovation clearly grew out of his own Council during the last decade of Edward's reign. But in another sense it represented a significant break with the past. The Duke of Gloucester's authority sprang from the fact that he was a great landowner in the North, while Lincoln was a royal official, appointed to serve at the king's pleasure.

With the North in safe hands Richard found time in August to spend a few weeks in London, which he had not visited since he left the capital in March. During this stay, he had the bones of Henry VI transferred from Chertsey to their final resting place in St George's Chapel at Windsor. Some said that this was a spiteful move to put an end to the pilgrimages made to his tomb. But it was more likely an act of conventional piety and even his enemy John Rous conceded that the ceremony was conducted with the greatest solemnity.

By 11 September the king had returned to Nottingham, where he received the Scottish ambassadors in great state. The embassy included the Earl of Argyll, Chancellor of Scotland, the Bishop of Aberdeen, Lord Lisle and a train of clerics, heralds and attendants. In the great hall of Nottingham Castle, they were greeted by Richard and his Chancellor, the Duke of Norfolk, the Earl of Northumberland, Lord Stanley, the two Chief Justices and the principal officers of the royal household. Before the commissioners got down to business the Archdeacon of Lothian, who was also James III's secretary, delivered a lengthy panegyric in Latin on Richard's virtues. Never, according to the Archdeacon, had nature endowed a small frame with so great a soul and such strength of mind. Ten days later, the negotiators had completed their discussion. There was to be a three-year truce, and James's heir, the Duke of Rothesay, was to marry Richard's niece, Anne de la Pole. With the back door to his kingdom sealed by a treaty of friendship and marriage, Richard was free at last to concentrate his efforts on Henry Tudor.

The threat of invasion was, in fact, receding. October was too late to contemplate a military campaign, and the realm was safe until the following spring. Nevertheless, Richard sat out the whole of the month of October on the black rock of Nottingham, before returning to his capital. 'On the eleventh day of November', recorded Robert Fabyan, 'the mayor and his brethren, being clad in scarlet, and the citizens to the number of five hundred or more, in violet, met the king beyond Kingston in Southwark and so brought him to the Wardrobe, beside the Black Friars.'

Since his surrender at St Michael's Mount nearly

ten years previously, John de Vere, Earl of Oxford, had been imprisoned in the great fortress of Hammes that guarded Calais. But, with Henry Tudor at the French Court, Richard had taken the precaution of ordering Oxford's transfer to an English prison. His suspicions were only too well-founded, for now he learned that Oxford had persuaded his gaoler, James Blount, to turn his coat, and the pair of them had fled to Paris. Some of the smaller fry were less fortunate. Late in November Richard laid his hands on William Colyngbourne, a former servant of Cecily Neville, the king's mother, who had been sending messages to Henry Tudor. Evidently he had a sense of humour too, for it was he who penned the rhyme about the Cat, the Rat, the Dog and the Hog. Richard determined to make an example of the rhymester, who was tried at the Guildhall early in December and condemned to a traitor's death. 'For the which he was drawn unto the Tower Hill and there full cruelly put to death, at first hanged and straight cut down and ripped, and his bowels cast into a fire. The which torment was so speedily done that when the butcher pulled out his heart he spake and said JESUS, JESUS.'

Treason was in the air. In an atmosphere of deepening mistrust and suspicion Richard gave out fresh proclamations against his rival's claims, renewed the commissions of array first issued in May, and authorised the commissioners to summon 'the knights, squires and gentlemen within the said counties, and know from them what number of people, defensibly arrayed, every of them severally will bring at half a day's warning, if any sudden arrival fortune of the king's rebels and traitors'. Harwich was reinforced with a strong royal garrison, and the faithful Sir James Tyrell was sent across the Channel to assume command of the castle of Guisnes. To preserve an outward façade of strength and confidence, Christmas was celebrated at Westminster with the magnificence of a second coronation. But, behind the show of 'dancing and gaiety and many vain changes of apparel', Richard was champing for action. The strain of waiting was beginning to affect his purse as well as his nerve. The careful administration of the royal estates covered the normal expenses of his household in peace time: but it

Fifteenth-century long-toed leather shoe, known as a 'crocowe' or 'pomaine'.

could not generate the huge sums of ready cash needed to maintain a permanent state of military alert.

The best news that reached Richard at Christmas 1484 came from his agents in France: the Lancastrian invasion was definitely scheduled for the following summer. At last the issue would be decided one way or the other.

Early in March 1485 another personal tragedy put a potent psychological weapon into Henry Tudor's hands. Queen Anne was dying, wasted by a disease her doctors declared to be mortal and highly infectious. On the 16th, 'upon the day of the great eclipse of the sun, Queen Anne departed this life and was buried at Westminster with no less honours than befitted the interment of a queen'. The rumour-mongers lost no time in getting to work: Richard himself was said to have poisoned the Queen who could bear him no more children. Worse still, he now planned to gratify an incestuous passion for his niece, Elizabeth of York. Such a marriage would, of course, have scuppered Henry's prospects. But it made no sense for Richard to marry the lady himself. His own claims to the throne were founded on the theory that all Edward IV's children were bastards. But the rumours stuck. Had the king not equipped his niece with gowns as magnificent as the Queen's during the recent Christmas festivities, and avoided his wife's bedside as she lay dying? Henry's supporters were probably genuinely frightened that the match might take place, and did all in their power to promote the scandal as a means of preventing it. Even the faithful Cat and Rat were persuaded to subscribe to the rumours, and bluntly informed their master that the country – particularly the North – would not stand for it. Twelve doctors of divinity were paraded to tell Richard that the Pope would not grant him the necessary dispensation. By these tactics the king was eventually manœuvred into making the public denial the Lancastrians were hoping for. At the Hospital of the Knights of St John, in Clerkenwell, the Mayor and Aldermen heard from the king's own lips that the marriage had never crossed his mind. At the same time he wrote to the Mayor of York advising him to pay no heed to the 'divers seditious and evilly disposed persons' who 'enforce themselves daily to sow seeds of noise and slander against our person'.

Those evilly-disposed persons were doubtless also complaining loudly of Richard's financial exactions. The treasure bequeathed by Edward IV had all been spent in the suppression of Buckingham's rebellion and in the preparations of the previous summer. A pliant Parliament could usually be cajoled into granting a subsidy, but such taxes took a long time to collect. There was no alternative but to revert to the benevolences that caused so much unfavourable comment in Edward's day. Since Richard had gone out of his way to condemn benevolences in Parliament only twelve months before, their renewal caused widespread resentment. Nevertheless, between

February and April his commissioners managed to scrape together some £20,000.

The great guessing game was about to begin. Where would Henry land and when would he come? Richard was not inclined to take any chances, and in June he once again took up his watch at the castle of Nottingham. His most able lieutenants were disposed in a great area covering the coasts from Essex to North Wales. The south-east was entrusted to Norfolk and his son the Earl of Surrey. Sir Robert Brackenbury, Constable of the Tower, took charge of London's defences. In Southampton harbour a well-equipped naval squadron lay at Viscount Lovell's command. The Tudors' family connections with South Wales and the lordship of Pembroke called for special defences in that area. William Herbert, Earl of Huntingdon, held Carmarthen and Brecon; Richard Williams held the strongholds of Pembroke, Tenby and Haverfordwest; and James Tyrell's men garrisoned Builth and Llandovery. On the adjoining hills beacons were laid, ready to flash across the valleys the news of Henry's coming.

On 22 June Richard put his commissioners of array on special alert. 'In all haste possible' they were to 'review the soldiers late mustered, and see that they be able persons well horsed and harnessed to do the king service, and if they be not, to put other able men in their places.' They were to be ready to move at an hour's warning 'upon peril of losing their lives, lands and goods'. At the same time the propaganda war was stepped up with another proclamation: the Lancastrian rebels were in the pocket of the king's ancient enemies, the French, to whom they had pledged the towns of Calais, Guisnes and Hammes. Their leader was one Henry Tudor, of bastard blood on his mother's side as on his father's. If his cause prospered, this same Henry planned to strip the king's subjects bare in order to reward the traitors, adulterers and extortioners who followed him.

Despite these energetic preparations, Richard knew well that the issue could turn on the loyalty of a few men in high places. One such man was Thomas, Lord Stanley, who sought the king's permission in July to visit his family in Lancashire. As Steward of Richard's Household, Stanley had spent the best part of the last two years at the king's side, and was associated with him in all the principal acts of his reign. But he was also married to Henry Tudor's mother, Margaret Beaufort, the Countess of Richmond. It was an awkward dilemma: assent – and risk that Stanley would lead his 3,000 Lancashiremen to Henry's camp; deny – and risk a mortal insult to the man who had taken Richard's part against his own Countess in 1483. Never at his best when it came to diplomacy, Richard settled on a compromise that invited both the treason and the insult. Stanley was allowed to go, providing he sent his eldest son, Lord Strange, to Nottingham in his place.

The waiting was now almost done. On 24 July informants brought word from France that Tudor was making ready to embark at Harfleur. The Master of Rolls was quickly sent to London to fetch the Great Seal of England. On the same day that the Seal was delivered to the king at Nottingham, the rebel ships slipped their moorings and hoisted sail for the Welsh coast.

7
Bosworth

1484–5

With the help of fair weather and 'A soft southern wind', Henry Tudor, Earl of Richmond landed at Milford Haven in the county of Pembroke at sunset on 7 August. Nearly half of his twenty-six years had been spent in exile. It was his first visit to the land of his fathers since his uncle Jasper Tudor, Earl of Pembroke, had taken him abroad following the Lancastrian débâcle at Tewkesbury in 1471. With a proper sense of occasion, and a shrewd eye for propaganda, Henry's first recorded act was to kneel down and kiss the sands of Mill Bay.

The army he brought from France was hardly impressive. Jasper Tudor and the Earl of Oxford were the only two men of any consequence. Edward Woodville represented the family of his prospective bride. The rest of the English contingent were mainly the attainted rebels of Buckingham's abortive rebellion – Richard Guildford, John Cheyney, William Brandon, William Berkeley and a few others. The 2,000 soldiers at his back were French convicts, persuaded to enlist by the promise of a free pardon. But it was not on them that Henry pinned his hopes. Since the early spring, his messengers had been sounding out possible sympathisers, rekindling the embers of Lancastrian loyalism, promising lands and titles to those who would betray their oaths to King Richard. In Wales especially the seeds of treason had fallen on fertile ground. The Tudors were known in Wales, while the Yorkist kings were foreigners. As his banner Henry chose the red dragon of the old Welsh kings, from whom he claimed his descent.

On 8 August Henry marched unopposed into the county town of Haverfordwest. A delegation from the town of Pembroke arrived to pledge its allegiance. Rumours that Sir Walter Herbert from Carmarthen was approaching with a large troop loyal to the king proved groundless. As Henry marched north through Cardigan and Aberystwyth to Merioneth, the towns and fortresses whose loyalty Richard had been at such pains to insure opened their gates to welcome his rival. From Merioneth his line of march swung to the east, through Newton and the Vale of Powys to the borders of Shropshire. Here he was joined by 'a great baulk of soldiers' under the black raven banner of Rhys ap Thomas, the Welsh chieftain who had promised Richard that the Tudor would cross the mountains into England only over his dead body. Shrewsbury opened its gates to the invader on 15 August. Pushing on to Newport the next day, Henry's growing band of French and Welsh was joined by 500 Shropshiremen under Sir Gilbert Talbot.

Thus far the enterprise had prospered. But Henry was in England now, less than sixty miles from Richard's crag at Nottingham, and still his step-father, Lord Stanley, had not joined him. So much depended on the notorious trimmer and on his scarcely less powerful brother Sir William, who held North Wales and much of Shropshire. At Stafford, on 17 August, Henry had

The red dragon of Wales, one of the heraldic supporters of Henry VII's arms from King's College Chapel, Cambridge. Henry chose the dragon as his symbol because of its associations with the old Welsh kings.

his first meeting with Sir William. King Richard, he was told, held Stanley's son, Lord Strange, a hostage at Nottingham. If the brothers declared for Henry now, he would surely lose his head. Glibly Sir William unfolded his strategy: Lord Stanley's army, presently encamped at Lichfield only fifteen miles away, would retreat before Henry's line of march until Richard's forces blocked the way. Richard himself would suspect nothing until the battle commenced, and Stanley's men fell on his unguarded flank. As proof of the Stanleys' good faith, Sir William arranged a secret *rendezvous* between Henry and his brother at the village of Atherstone, south-east of Lichfield astride the old Roman road of Watling Street. It was a neat plan, but Henry saw that, when it came to the battle, his own flank would be as vulnerable as Richard's.

By this time Richard had received an equally ambiguous token of Lord Stanley's intentions. The couriers who rode from Pembroke with the news of Henry's landing reached Nottingham three days later, on 11 August. His army, they reported, was pitifully small and ill-equipped. In the words of Henry VIII's historian, Edward Hall, this intelligence 'so inflated Richard's mind, that in a manner disdaining to here speak of so poor a company, [he] determined at first to take little or no regard to this so small a sparkle, declaring the earl [of Richmond] to be innocent and unwise because that he temerariously attempted such a great enterprise with so small and thin a number of warlike persons'. His Welsh captains, Sir

Walter Herbert and Rhys ap Thomas, would doubtless put the invader to 'shameful confusion'. All the same if Henry did emerge from his Welsh mountains, the opportunity to come to grips with the man who had kept Richard on the hook for the past two years was not to be missed. The king therefore lost no time in summoning his captains to his side – Northumberland from his manor of Wressell, Norfolk and Surrey from Essex, Lovell from Southampton, Brackenbury from London and Thomas, Lord Stanley from his Lancashire estates. The royal army would muster further south at Leicester, poised to intercept the Lancastrians if they planned a march on London.

In the event, the shameful confusion was not Henry's but Richard's. For on Monday 15 August his mounted scouts or 'scurriers' brought word that the Earl of Richmond had crossed the Severn at Shrewsbury and was heading in a straight line for Nottingham, his forces swollen by the Welsh levies raised to stop him. 'At which message,' according to Hall, 'he was sore moved and broiled with melancholy and dolour, and cried out, asking vengeance on them that contrary to their oath and promise had fraudulently deceived him.' Resisting the impulse to set out, as originally planned, on the following day, the king had to kick his heels for four more days, waiting for his army to reach its full strength.

More ominous news followed shortly. A message from Lord Stanley regretfully announced that the Steward was too sick with the sweating sickness to obey the king's summons. Fearing Richard's vengeance, Lord Strange tried to slip away from the castle. When he was apprehended in the nick of time, Strange confessed under interrogation that he, his uncle Sir William and Sir John Savage were indeed conspiring to ally themselves with Henry Tudor. But he would not implicate his father.

Rhys ap Thomas, Walter Herbert, Talbot and now Stanley – a fog of treason was closing in around Richard's well-laid martial plans. On Tuesday the 17th, as he sought to relieve the tensions of his enforced idleness by hunting in Sherwood Forest, two messengers from York arrived to cast doubts on Northumberland's loyalty too. Having learned of Henry's landing, the city fathers were anxious to know why the commissioners of array had not called on the men of York to send armed help to their King. Perhaps the reason was the plague that had recently swept the city. Or was Northumberland trying to restrict the levy to his own retainers, men who would put their loyalty to the House of Percy above their allegiance to the reigning House of York?

Late on Thursday the 18th the Lancastrian army was reported to have changed its line of march. Turning south-east from Stafford towards Lichfield, Henry's van now seemed to be headed not towards Nottingham, but towards Atherstone where Lord Stanley lay, and the main highway to London. Even if his muster was not yet complete, Richard had to act now. The following morning the royal army, marching four abreast, left Nottingham by the southern gate and took the road for Leicester. 'With a frowning countenance and truculent aspect' Richard rode at the centre of the column, mounted on a great white courser, the yeomen of the Crown before him and wings of cavalry at his flanks. By 9 o'clock that same evening the king was at Leicester at an inn that displayed his own sign of the White Boar. The two halves of Richard's host were now united: together with Northumberland's contingent, which was expected within the next twenty-four hours, they appear to have numbered more than ten thousand men. 'Here', states the Croyland Chronicle, 'was found a number of warriors ready to fight on the king's side, greater than had ever been seen before in England collected together in behalf of one person.'

This was, of course, an exaggeration, but Henry Tudor was heavily outnumbered all the same. His recruiting drive in Wales and Shropshire had added about three thousand men to the two thousand who landed at Milford Haven. Without the certainty of Stanley's support his prospects seemed decidedly bleak. The mass desertions confidently predicted by his agents in the spring had simply not materialised.

Distracted by these unpalatable thoughts, Henry apparently paused by the roadside on the evening of the 19th while his army marched on to Tamworth. The only others with him were a bodyguard of about twenty armed men. When night closed in he was shocked to discover, in Vergil's words, that 'he could not discern the trace of them that were gone before, and so, after long wandering could not find his company, he came unto a certain town [village] more than three miles from his camp, full of fear; who lest he might be betrayed, durst not ask questions of any man, but tarried there all night', as fearful of the present as he was of the perils to come. Reunited with his army on the morning of the 20th, Henry blandly assured his anxious followers that he had slipped away on purpose 'to receive some good news of his secret friends'.

20 August was in fact the day appointed for Henry's secret *rendezvous* with the Stanleys at Atherstone, some eight miles beyond Tamworth and barely twenty miles from Richard's host at Leicester. Vergil's details of this meeting are sparse, but they do indicate that it went some way to allaying Henry's doubts about his step-father: 'taking one another by the hand, and yielding mutual salutation, each man was glad for the good state of the others, and all their minds were moved to great joy. After that they entered in counsel in what sort to arraign battle with King Richard if the matter should come to strokes.' When the conference was over, Lord Stanley withdrew his troops to Stoke Golding and Henry's army took over Atherstone.

That same evening at Leicester, King Richard conducted a final review of his troops. All the most important Yorkist leaders were with him now, including the two late arrivals, Northumberland and Brackenbury.

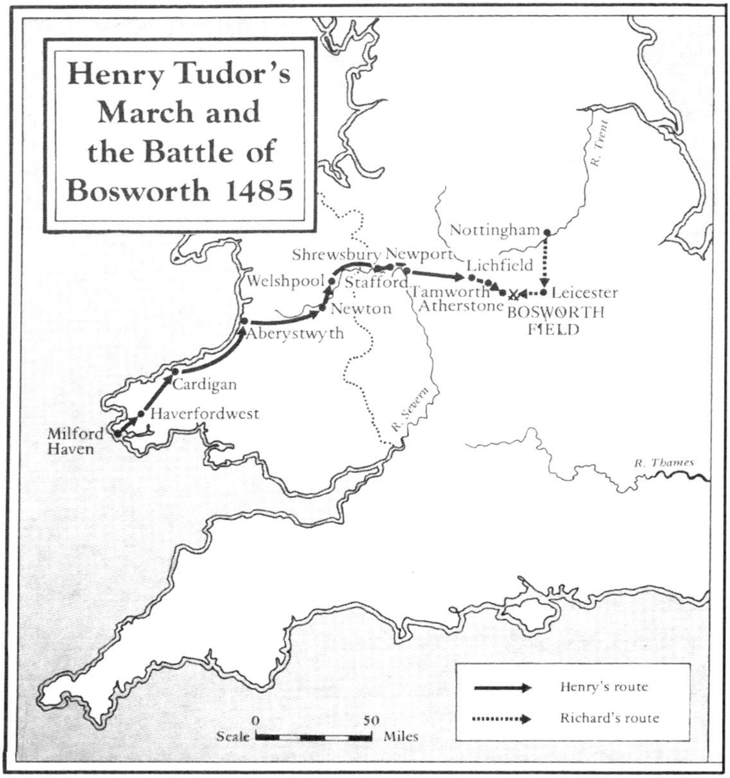

Early on Sunday morning a vanguard of archers and men at arms, wearing the silver lion badges of the Duke of Norfolk, led the royal army west towards the Lancastrian camp at Atherstone. The two armies would not clash on a Sunday, but Richard was anxious to narrow the gap as much as possible, both to forestall a Lancastrian dash down Watling Street, and to establish visual contact with the two forces led by the Stanley brothers. Twelve miles from Leicester, just beyond the village of Sutton Cheney, he found a position ideal for his purpose. Overlooking Redmore Plain, Sutton Cheney stood on high ground at the eastern end of a ridge, about one and a half miles to the west of Sir William Stanley's camp at Shenton, and just over two miles north of Lord Stanley at Stoke Golding. Less than three miles beyond Stoke Golding lay Watling Street, the highway to London.

As the afternoon wore on, Richard's scouts informed him that the Earl of Richmond's van had left Watling Street and taken the old Roman road towards Redmore Plain, soon to be renamed Bosworth Field. The long wait was over. Henry Tudor had decided to commit his cause to the test of arms. That night the campfires of Richard's enemies lit up the sky less than three miles from the king's tent.

Predictably enough, our two contemporary voices – Croyland and Vergil – attribute to Richard a sleepless night, interrupted by 'dreadful visions' and premonitions of disaster. At daybreak, says the Croyland Chronicler, his drawn features were even more livid and ghastly than usual. Moreover 'there were no chaplains present to perform divine service on behalf of King Richard, nor any breakfast prepared to refresh the flagging spirits of the king'. If he did indeed dispense with early morning Mass and breakfast, it was because a vital strategic manœuvre had to be performed before the Lancastrians stirred from their bivouacs. This was the occupation of Ambien Hill, the western end of the ridge on which Sutton Cheney stood. Ambien Hill jutted out some four hundred feet above the level of Redmore Plain: on its northern side the steep slopes would protect the right flank against Sir William Stanley's men, just as the swampy ground on the gentler southern slopes would deter his brother from an attempt on Richard's left.

As the Lancastrian van, under the Earl of Oxford, skirted the swamp and moved towards Ambien's western slopes, they were greeted by the sight of Norfolk's men already ensconced on the brow of the ridge above them. The archers crouched in the front ranks, equipped with their six-foot longbows of yew, oak or maplewood. The longbow, with a range of up to two hundred and fifty yards, was still the favoured weapon of the common soldier, and an expert could discharge a dozen arrows within a single minute. However, since the end of the wars in France the general level of expertise had declined – so much so that in 1478 an act of Parliament specifically outlawed football and other frivolous pastimes, which were held responsible for the decline. Like the archers, the ordinary infantrymen drawn behind carried swords at their sides, but their main weapon was a stout wooden pike, about the same length as the longbow and tipped with a heavy metal spearhead for jabbing their victims to death. The common soldier was lightly armoured, if at all. His tunic, or jack, was made up from layers of boiled hide, stuffed with hemp to give added protection. It was said that an

English jack, which reached down to its owner's thighs, could stop an arrow or a swordthrust more effectively than a knight's hauberk of chain mail. On his head the common soldier wore a sallett, or plain metal helmet, without a vizor to protect his eyes and face.

The cream of Richard's army were his men-at-arms. They had come to the battlefield mounted, but they would fight on foot, clustered round the pennons of the simple knights, or the more gorgeous silken banners of the knights banneret to whom they were bound by their contracts of indenture. There was a gesture of bravado in this tradition – as in the story that the Earl of Warwick slew his horse on the eve of the Battle of Towton, swearing that he would not live to run away. Less nimble than the common soldier, the man-at-arms was encased from the waist up in two metal plates, one to guard his chest, the other his back. He carried a variety of weapons – sword, dagger, pike, battleaxe or the formidable halberd that could stab like a pike or be swung like an axe. A few were equipped with firearms of wrought iron or brass, but loading the lead pellets was a cumbersome business and they were of little use when it came to hand-to-hand fighting.

Seven thousand men or more were stretched along the top of the ridge, from the summit of Ambien Hill to the outskirts of Sutton Cheney where the line was anchored by Northumberland's rearguard of 3,000. At the centre of the vanguard a knot of horsemen under

Arms and Armour at the time of Bosworth

The knights who fought for Richard III and Henry Tudor at the Battle of Bosworth Field wore plate-armour, riveted at the joints. Plate provided protection against sword and lance thrusts, and to a certain extent against primitive firearms, but was extremely bulky and uncomfortable to wear. Knights would carry swords, daggers and battle-axes.

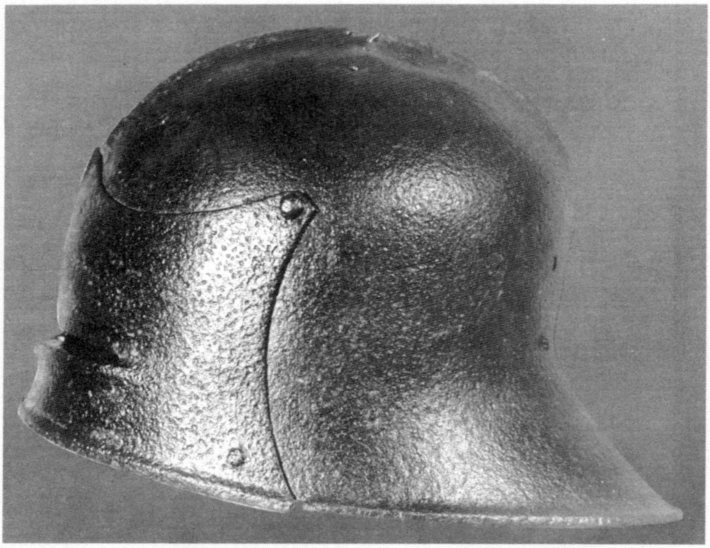

A sallett, a plain metal helmet, dating from 1460. The rear of the sallett was shaped in such a way as to protect the neck.

A 15th-century depiction of jousting in a tournament, taken from a Book of Hours.

Men-at-arms wore armour to protect only the upper parts of their bodies, while common soldiers usually depended for protection upon tunics of leather stuffed with hemp, for they had to be agile in battle. On their heads they would wear salletts, and they would carry a variety of staff weapons, including pikes and halberds.

the banner of the silver lion signalled the presence of the Duke of Norfolk, his son Thomas, Earl of Surrey and his chief lieutenants, Lords Zouche and Ferrers. At the centre of the ridge, a larger mounted concourse marked the king himself, surrounded by his close advisers Lovell, Ratcliffe and Catesby, by the knights and esquires of his bodyguard, and by the men who led the contingents of the North and Midlands, Lords Dacre, Graystoke and Scrope of Bolton.

Richard's mood was both determined and resigned. In Vergil's words: 'Knowing certainly that that day would either yield him a peaceable and quiet realm from thenceforth or else perpetually bereave him of the same, he came to the field with the crown upon his head, that thereby he might either make a beginning or end of his reign.' From his own bitter experience he knew that war was no chivalric adventure, as recounted in the ballads of Crécy and Agincourt. If he won, he told his captains, he meant to crush every one of the rebels marching under Henry's banners. If he lost, Henry would do the same to them. In this spirit he sent his last message to Lord Stanley. Declare for Richard now, or Lord Strange would be instantly beheaded. Back came the answer that Lord Stanley had other sons, and would not join the king. Either because Richard relented when his bluff was called, or because his orders were disobeyed, Lord Strange survived his ordeal.

As the gap between the opposing vanguards narrowed,

Henry Tudor too sent a last appeal to Lord Stanley, whose men were moving slowly forward towards the swamp. Would he now join forces with Oxford in the assault on Ambien Hill? Stanley still hesitated. He would make his own dispositions, and join his stepson when the time was ripe. The trimmer's steadfast refusal to declare himself left Henry, in Vergil's words, 'no little vexed', but he was now too far committed to draw back. With Talbot's Shropshiremen on his right and Sir John Savage commanding the Welshmen on his left, Oxford planned to throw the entire Lancastrian army into the attack. Henry, who had no experience of war, would remain in the rear, protected by a slender screen of footmen and a single troop of horse.

The rebel troops reached the lower slopes and began to climb. As soon as they were within range Norfolk's troops unleashed a shower of arrows. Then Norfolk's trumpets sounded the order to charge, and the royal army streamed down the slopes. The Lancastrians were under strict orders not to stray more than a few feet from the standards of their company commanders. Under the shock of Norfolk's charge, Oxford's close-packed formations wavered but did not break. All around the lower slopes of Ambien Hill, the two front lines were locked in fierce hand-to-hand combat. Slowly at first, the Yorkists began to give ground. Norfolk himself thrust his way to the front in the effort to rally his men. Then disaster struck. Norfolk was down. Soon his men were in full retreat towards the top of the hill. Richard immediately gave orders for Northumberland to bring up his rearguard. But Henry Percy, taking his cue from Lord Stanley, had no intention of risking his neck in the dynastic blood feud that had already killed his father and his grandfather. When the battle was over, he would give his allegiance to the victor. Politely but firmly he let Richard know that he would stay put, to guard against a possible move by Lord Stanley's men.

The situation was dangerous but not desperate. The vanguard was badly mauled, but the Yorkist centre was still intact. Northumberland refused to move for Richard, but neither of the Stanleys had yet moved against him.

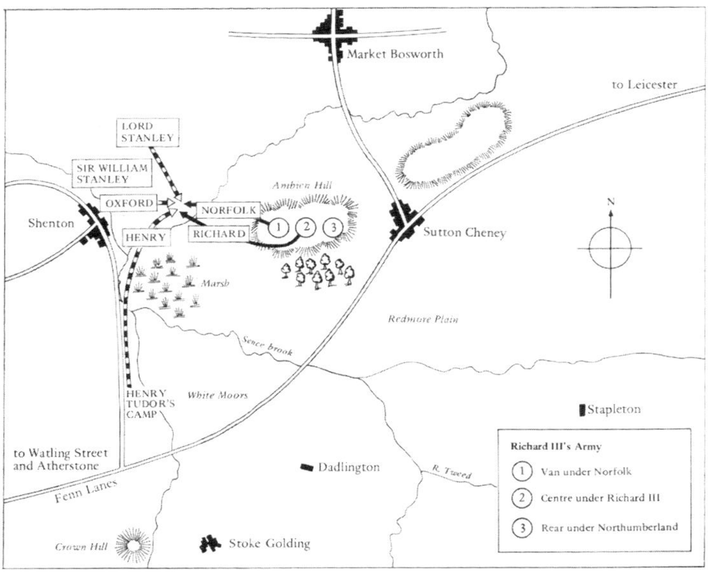

Nonetheless Richard was too impatient to let the grim mêlée on Ambien Hill decide the day. While his best captain lay dead, the king's sword was still unblooded. The morale of his personal followers was sinking. Some faint hearts suggested flight: in the North there were still plenty of able-bodied men who would take his part against Henry Tudor.

Abruptly, Richard came to his decision. Less than a mile off on Redmore Plain his scouts had spotted the red dragon banner of his rival, screened by the small rearguard that Oxford had detached from his main force. If he could despatch Henry Tudor, the battle would be over. More than that, Henry's death would settle for ever the bloody feud between Lancaster and York. The orders were quickly given. At the head of his household knights and squires of the body – Sir Richard Ratcliffe, Hugh and Thomas Stafford, Sir Robert Brackenbury, Sir Robert Percy, Sir Ralph Assheton and about eighty others – Richard rode forward, skirting the battle on his left, down the north-western slope of Ambien Hill, and thundered out across the plain. His route took him straight across the path of Sir William Stanley, whom he had proclaimed a traitor less than a week before. As Sir William's men struggled into their saddles, Richard's cavalry crashed into the enemy ranks. The impetus of the charge carried them straight through the protective screen of infantry. Making straight for his target the king slew the Earl of Richmond's standard bearer, Sir William Brandon, with his own hand, and unhorsed the bulky figure of Sir John Cheyney who came to Brandon's aid. For a moment it seemed as if the king's desperate enterprise was about to be crowned with success.

But already Sir William Stanley's horsemen were colliding with the rear of Richard's little force. As the ring of steel closed in around him, Richard was overwhelmed and battered to the ground. John Rous, who had no cause to bless Richard's memory, had this to say of his last moments: 'If I may speak the truth to his honour, although small of body and weak in strength, he most valiantly defended himself as a noble knight to his last breath, often exclaiming as he was betrayed, and saying – Treason! Treason! Treason!'

After the battle Richard's body was recovered from the corpses piled around Henry's fallen banner and stripped of all its clothing. With a halter around the neck the naked corpse was strung across the back of a pack horse and taken off to Leicester. Here it lay exposed for two days, as proof of Henry's triumph, before it was buried without ceremony in the chapel of the Greyfriars. The tomb to which Henry contributed the sum of £10–15 was destroyed at the dissolution of the monasteries, and Richard's bones were thrown into the River Soar.

8

Scorpio Ascendant

1485

Although he reigned only two years and two months, Richard is assured of immortality. He was the last English king to die in battle, the last of the Plantagenet line of kings, and the date of his death is said to mark the close of that otherwise indefinable episode known as the Middle Ages. Above all, he is the chief suspect in the longest and most emotive murder trial in English history.

Oddly enough, it was the imaginative efforts of the Tudor historians to blacken his name that most effectively ensured lasting fame and the great debate that continues to this day. Henry VII, and his son Henry VIII after him, were always naggingly conscious of the flaws in their hereditary claims to the Crown. The Tudors were therefore particularly susceptible to the flattery of the propagandists who portrayed Richard as an inhuman tyrant, hunch-backed, treacherous and cruel, and who contrasted the dark winter of the House of York with the spring sunshine of the first Tudors. The first man to contribute to this tradition – a Warwickshire priest with antiquarian interests named John Rous – is especially interesting because he wrote both before and after Bosworth. His best-known work is an illustrated history of the earls of Warwick, which survives in two copies, one in English and the other in Latin, both of which were completed before 1485. In the English version Richard is described as 'a mighty prince and especial good lord... in his realm full commendably punishing offenders

Stained-glass portrait of Richard III, from the parish church at Penrith, one of Richard's principal estates in the North.

of the laws, especially oppressors of the Commons, and cherishing those that were virtuous, by the which discreet guiding he got great thanks and love of all his subjects great and poor'. In the Latin version, which was presumably still in the author's possession in August 1485, this passage is edited out and Richard appears simply as 'the unhappy husband' of Anne Neville. Sometime before his death in 1491, Rous also compiled a *History of the Kings of England,* which he dedicated to Henry VII. The venomous flavour of this tract can be judged from the statement that Richard was born, after two years in his mother's womb, with a complete set of teeth, and hair down to his shoulders. 'At whose birth', Rous continues, 'Scorpio was in the ascendant, which sign is in the House of Mars; and as a scorpion mild in countenance, stinging in the tail, so he showed himself to all.'

Neither Rous's monster nor the 'serpent swollen with rage' and 'thirster after human blood' depicted in *The Life of Henry VII* by Prince Arthur's blind tutor, Bernard André, were sufficiently subtle or convincing for Henry's taste. In the last years of his reign he decided to commission a history of England from an Italian scholar trained in the Classical traditions of Renaissance humanism. Polydore Vergil's *History,* first published in 1534, was designed for the consumption of courts and scholars, and avoids the crude invective of his predecessors. The overall argument is that the Wars of the Roses were a divine punishment visited on the kingdom as a result of the original sin of Henry IV's usurpation in 1399, culminating in the tyranny of Richard's reign and eventually purged through Henry VII's union of Lancaster with York. In order to lend substance to this theme Vergil deftly adds to the list of Richard's villainies several new accusations, always safeguarding his integrity with the qualifications that he is reporting popular beliefs. Thus Gloucester is portrayed, along with Clarence, actually stabbing Henry VI's son Edward to death after the Battle of Tewkesbury. Of Henry VI's death in the Tower he declares 'the continual report is that Richard, Duke of Gloucester, killed him with a sword whereby his brother might be delivered of all hostility'.

But the most influential account of Richard to

appear in the early sixteenth century was Sir Thomas More's incomplete *History of King Richard III,* written in about 1513. Ironically, More's book, which ends with Buckingham's rebellion, was never intended for publication, nor was its primary aim to glorify the Tudor dynasty. More saw Richard as the antithesis of the humanist vision of a Good Prince, a symbol of evil rather than a person of flesh and blood, his crippled body a mirror image of his twisted soul: 'Malicious, wrathful, envious', 'little of stature, ill featured of limbs, crook backed', 'close and secret, a deep dissimuler, lowly of countenance, arrogant of heart, outwardly companionable where he inwardly hated, not letting to kiss whom he thought to kill', 'he slew with his own handes king Henry the Sixth', and 'lacked not in helping forth his brother Clarence to his death'. After doing away with the princes in the tower Richard 'never had quiet in his mind', 'so was his restless heart continually tossed and tumbled with the tedious impression and stormy remembrance of his abominable deed'.

Vergil and More provided the inspiration for all the later Tudor versions, including the chronicles of Edward Hall (1548), Richard Grafton (1568) and Raphael Holinshed (1578), and culminating in the 'poisonous hunchbacked toad' of Shakespeare's great melodrama.

Inevitably, such absurd exaggerations have provoked a flood of counter-claims in Richard's favour. Not long after the last of the Tudors was in her grave, Sir George

Buc, James I's Master of the Revels, set to work on a five-volume biography, whose theme is that Richard's 'wisdom and courage had not then their nickname and calumny as now, but drew the eyes and acknowledgment of the whole kingdom towards him'. A more important milestone in Richard's rehabilitation is Horace Walpole's *Historic Doubts,* which argues most persuasively on the grounds of common sense that 'many of the crimes imputed to Richard seemed impossible; and, what was stronger, contrary to his interest'. At the end of the nineteenth century, Sir Clements Markham ingeniously turned the tables on Richard's conqueror by accusing Henry VII of the murder of the princes. Markham's theories, which have been generally discounted since the analysis of the skeletons from the Tower, underline an important point about almost everything that has been written on Richard's life and reign: that the king's guilt or innocence in the murder of the princes is an acceptable yardstick whereby we can judge everything else that he did. Fuelled with moral outrage, the hostile critic sees in every act of justice a cynical attempt to cultivate popularity; in every grant a bribe; in every gesture of conciliation the stirrings of an uneasy conscience. As recently as 1966 the All Souls antiquarian A. L. Rowse declared that 'anyone deriving his view of the whole story from Shakespeare would not be far out'; compared the execution of Lord Hastings with Hitler's Night of the Long Knives; and with a logic worthy of his fifteenth-century namesake John Rous, cites Henry's barbarous treatment of his rival's corpse as proof of Richard's villainy.

Even if we do succeed in peeling off the layers of prejudice, it is still not easy to arrive at a true assessment of Richard's character. His life coincides with a particularly barren patch as far as contemporary historians go. Most of the major events in his reign have to be reconstructed from unreliable Lancastrian or Tudor sources whose bias is manifest. Even his physical appearance is elusive. His portraits show him with a rather careworn expression, thin pursed lips, brown eyes, a thrusting jaw and delicate tapering fingers. According to Sir Thomas More, who comments favourably on the good looks of Edward and Clarence, Richard was 'little of stature, ill featured of limbs, crook backed, his left shoulder much higher than his right'. This disparity of the shoulders, which John Rous also mentions, appears to be the sole foundation for the later myth of the ugly, hunchbacked cripple. The Elizabethan antiquarian John Stow specifically discounts the myth on the evidence of 'ancient men' who testified that Richard was quite handsome, although a little below average height. Horace Walpole repeats an anecdote that the Countess of Desmond, after dancing with Richard, declared him to be the handsomest man in the room excepting his brother Edward. There is disagreement even about his height. The Scottish orator of 1484 made reference to Richard's shortness in his speech of address: yet the German diplomat Nicolas von Poppelau, who spent more than a week with the king at Middleham in May 1484, recorded that Richard was 'three fingers *taller* than himself, but a little slimmer, less thick set, and much more lean as well; he had delicate arms and legs, also a great heart'.

Nevertheless, there are sufficient grounds to rebuff or modify the outlines of the traditional Tudor villain. The most serious accusation – that he was consumed with ambition, 'a deep dissimuler' patiently waiting to snatch the reins of power from the fingers of his dead brother – has already been touched on in the preceding account of Richard's usurpation. His loyalty to Edward IV during his brother's lifetime is beyond dispute: as a devoted servant of the Crown Richard gains in stature from the contrast of Clarence's continual mischief-making. Nor could anyone have foretold that Edward's robust constitution would cave in at the age of forty. After Edward's death the Woodvilles showed themselves the first aggressors in their attempt to exclude the Duke of Gloucester from the position that was his by right of birth, by dint of his proven abilities and by the specific instructions Edward left in his will.

Nevertheless, the fact that Queen Elizabeth felt it necessary to safeguard her interests by forestalling Richard's protectorate shows that she had valid reasons to be afraid of him. The executions of Earl Rivers and Lord Richard Grey in late June 1483 bore out her misgivings. We know that Richard held her and her family responsible for Clarence's death, just as she had held Clarence responsible for her father's execution. But deeper motives were also at work. Mancini's reference to 'the good reputation' of Richard's private life supplies one clue. Richard's moral code is very succinctly expressed in a document addressed to his bishops in March 1484:

> Our principal intent and fervent desire is to see virtue and cleanness of living to be advanced... and vices... provoking the high indignation and fearful displeasure of God to be repressed and annulled; and this... put in execution by persons of lower degree to take thereof example... but also thereby the great and infinite goodness of God is made placable and graciously inclined to the exaudition of petitions and prayers.

This high moral tone – which Richard himself transgressed to the extent of fathering at least two bastards – reappears in a number of other State documents. The confirmation of his claim to the throne enacted by Parliament in 1484 speaks of 'every good maiden and woman standing in dread to be ravished and defouled' during Edward's reign. The inference is that Richard saw himself as the 'person of high estate' who would 'put in execution' the reign of virtue. The permissive atmosphere of Edward's Court seems, in Richard's eyes, to have been symptomatic of a deep-seated corruption stemming from his brother's adulterous liaison with Elizabeth Woodville and abetted by his brother's companions in vice, the Marquess of Dorset and Lord Hastings. Richard's vision of the Woodvilles and of Hastings as a gang of moral degenerates unfit to wield any form of temporal authority goes some way to explaining the vehemence of his retaliation. It also has ominous implications for Elizabeth's two sons, the unfortunate Princes.

This unattractive quirk of Richard's nature is well-attested by his treatment of Edward's favourite mistress, Jane Shore. This lady, who receives a glowing testimonial from Sir Thomas More, seems to have been quite free of the rapacity normally imputed to royal mistresses. 'The king would say that he had three concubines which in three divers properties diversely excelled: one the merriest, another the wiliest, the third the holiest harlot of his realm, as one whom no man could get out of the church lightly to any place, but it were to his bed.... But the merriest was this Shore's wife, in whom the king therefore took special pleasure, for many he had, but her he loved.'

When Edward died, Jane took up with Lord Hastings. The proclamation of Hastings's execution for treason made a special point of the fact that these two had spent the previous night in the same bed. Jane was sent to prison, had her possessions confiscated and was compelled to undergo public penance for harlotry. Shortly after the outbreak of Buckingham's rebellion in October 1483, 'the unshameful and mischievous woman called Shore's wife' crops up in another proclamation, this time as the mistress of the rebel Marquess of Dorset. Even when she was languishing in Ludgate prison, Richard continued to be obsessed by this unfortunate woman. On hearing a rumour that his own Solicitor-General, Thomas Lynom, intended to marry her, he wrote to the Lord Chancellor with instructions to 'exhort and stir him to the contrary'. Lynom took the hint and the marriage was called off.

Richard's puritanism had its positive side too. The minute attention he gave to the affairs of York, and the legislative programme of the 1484 Parliament both demonstrate his scrupulous regard for the welfare of his subjects. It is no coincidence that the two most enduring creations of his reign were concerned with the administration of justice. In December 1483, one John Harrington was appointed clerk of a sub-committee of the Council that met in the White Hall at Westminster to consider the 'bills, requests and supplications of poor persons'. From this developed the institution later known as the Court of Requests. The creation of the Council in the North in the following year was even more significant. It replaced the king's age-old dependence on feudal chieftains with a modern, streamlined replica of the parent Council at Westminster. The Tudors gratefully adopted the institution as their own, and it proved its value by outlasting the entire Tudor dynasty. It comes as no surprise that the Mayor and Aldermen of

York recorded the news of Bosworth with these words: 'King Richard, late mercifully reigning upon us, was... piteously slain and murdered, to the great heaviness of this city.'

In a letter excusing himself from an invitation to go hunting, Sir William Stanley – an older man than the king – writes that business is too pressing to get leave from 'Old Dick'. The epithet suggests that Richard, with his conscientious enthusiasm for the nuts and bolts of his administration, was regarded as a rather over-earnest plodder, well-intentioned, old-fashioned and a little dull. His private life, or rather the lack of it, supports this view. It gave rise to none of the colourful anecdotes that illumine the saintliness of Henry VI or the appetites of Edward IV. We know nothing about his relationship with Anne apart from the bare fact that they were both mad with grief at the death of her son. A single letter to his mother, Cecily, who was to outlive all her sons, suggests that he remained on polite but rather distant terms with her. The following letter, which concerns the appointment of a new steward to replace the treacherous William Colyngbourne, is the only one of Richard's family correspondence to survive:

> Madam, – I recommend me to you as heartily as is to me possible. Beseeching you in my most humble and affectuous wise of your daily blessing to my singular comfort and defence in my need. And,

> Madam, I heartily beseech you that I may often hear from you to my comfort. And such news as be here my servant Thomas Bryan, this bearer, shall show you to whom, please it you, to give credence unto. And, Madam, I beseech you to be good and gracious, Lady, to my Lord my chamberlain, to be your officer in Wiltshire in such as Collingbourne had. I trust he shall therein do you good service. And that it please you that by this bearer I may understand your pleasure in this behalf. And I pray God to send you the accomplishment of your noble desires. Written at Pomfret the 3rd day of June, 1484, with the hand of Your most humble son,
> Ricardus Rex.

Richard's favourite hobby was music. A foreign diplomat, Nicolas von Poppelau, who visited him at Pontefract or Middleham in May 1484, was greatly impressed by the singing at morning Mass. A gentleman of the royal chapel named John Melynek had earlier been commissioned to 'take and seize for the king all such singing men and children, being expert in the science of music, as he can find and think able to do the king's service within all places in the realm'. Able minstrels were also well rewarded, particularly those whom he was able to entice to his service from overseas. The king was also an enthusiastic builder, laying out considerable sums for altering and renovating the royal establishments of Windsor Castle, Westminster Palace, Baynard's Castle, the Tower of London, Nottingham Castle, the palace at York and the chapel at Pontefract. A gift of £300 went to the completion of King's College Chapel at Cambridge, and an annuity of 250 marks to St George's Chapel, Windsor. Even John Rous conceded that 'this King Richard is to be praised for his buildings'.

The two dominant strains in Richard's character – an assumption of moral superiority combined with a painstaking and conventional concept of duty – do resolve the puzzling contradictions touching on his personal code of honour. He could denounce the Treaty of Picquigny as a betrayal of chivalry and yet usurp the throne over the bodies of the rightful heirs. He could execute the Queen's brother, Earl Rivers, for treason, but he would not take the elementary precaution of marrying off the Queen's eldest daughter whose eligibility was so crucial to Henry Tudor's plans.

A 'thirster after blood' he was not. As Clarence's death shows, the steady escalation of violence and betrayal that characterises the Wars of the Roses coarsened Edward IV's amiable nature more than it did Richard's. Buckingham's rebellion was followed by less than a dozen executions, despite the fact that there was no pitched battle to take its toll of the king's enemies. The 95 attainders that followed compare favourably with the 113 enacted by Edward IV's Parliament after Towton in

1461. Neither Richard nor any of his servants exhibited the cold cruelty of Edward's Constable, John Tiptoft, Earl of Worcester, who was nicknamed the Butcher of England and himself went to the block in 1470 asking that his head should be severed with three strokes 'in honour of the Trinity'. If Richard had taken a tougher line with the rebel gentry of 1483, Henry would have had to do without a number of the men who joined him on the road to Bosworth. These conclusions portray a Richard very different from the exotic ogre conjured up by More and Shakespeare. Yet the fact remains that he was defeated and killed by a rival with a shaky claim to the throne, a hazy acquaintance with the country he was invading and an inferior army at his back. Why?

The major calamity of Richard's son's death in March 1484 undoubtedly played its part. After thirty years of intermittent civil war, invasions and depositions the majority of the gentry, merchants and yeomen classes were more interested in a settled succession than in the claims of the opposing branches of Edward III's quarrelsome family. When Prince Edward died there was little to choose between Richard and the unknown Welshman who had promised to marry Elizabeth of York.

Bad luck is only a part of the story. Despite the disappearance of so many famous names in the wars of Edward IV, it was still the élite of great magnates who decided the issue of who should be King, and it is his relationships with these men that reveal Richard's greatest failing. 'Old Dick', for all his solid virtues as an administrator and his undoubted courage on the battlefield, lacked Edward's knack of making friends. More's observation that he had a 'close and secret' nature hits on an uncomfortable truth. Perhaps it stemmed from a basic lack of self-confidence in dealing with people. He never felt at home in Edward's Court circle, distrusting both the easy familiarity of men like Hastings and Dorset, and the waves of intrigue emanating from the Queen's apartments. The extraordinary circumstances of Richard's upbringing cannot have failed to leave their mark on him, just as they did on his brother George. But whereas George's shallow nature gave way to a mixture of paranoia and bravado, Richard became wary, self-reliant and inaccessible. Louis XI, who was a shrewd judge of character, took an instant liking to Edward IV, but when he turned his charm on Richard of Gloucester he met with a total lack of response. Reserved and ill at ease with his peers, Richard chose to put his trust in boyhood friends such as Francis Lovell and Robert Percy, or able lieutenants, like Catesby and Ratcliffe, who owed their positions to his continuing favour. While he was Duke of Gloucester this self-sufficiency was a source of strength. But the king was a public figure whose words and gestures would be carefully marked. Richard's curt treatment of Louis eight years previously was returned with interest in the form of resolute hostility from the French.

The Tomb of Richard III in Leicester Cathedral.

Much more damaging were Richard's dealings with his own aristocracy. Temporarily dazzled by Buckingham he succeeded in driving Lord Hastings, his key supporter from the old régime, into the arms of the Woodville opposition. Henry Percy, his close associate in the North for more than ten years, was never cultivated. Lord Stanley was arrested, released, loaded with honours, kept close at heel for two years, then allowed to vanish to his estates on the eve of the Earl of Richmond's landing with polite threats of retribution on his son ringing in his ears. It is no coincidence that the only magnate whose loyalty Richard retained was the Duke of Norfolk, an old warhorse whose outlook was as blunt as his King's.

Richard was not, to his cost, a political animal. His penchant for direct action in place of patient diplomacy brought him to die in a battle that should never have taken place. Nevertheless, it is as well to remember that for all his political mistakes there was nothing pre-ordained about the Battle of Bosworth. With Northumberland and the Stanleys waiting on the sidelines, and Norfolk's troops matched against Oxford's, it was the superior generalship of the Lancastrian veteran and Richard's impromptu cavalry charge that decided the day. Nor did Bosworth represent the verdict of the majority of Richard's subjects. The general consensus of support that Richard enjoyed from his northern subjects, from his Commons in Parliament and from the country at large during Buckingham's rebellion did not evaporate mysteriously on Henry's landing.

In later years, Henry VII's subjects might reflect that the change of kings wrought few far-reaching changes in their prospects or conditions. The personal style of government inaugurated by Edward IV and inherited by Richard, the techniques of estate management applied to Crown lands, the abandonment of chauvinistic and chivalric adventures overseas, the fostering of commercial interests abroad and at home, and the erosion of baronial power are as characteristic of Henry Tudor's government as they were of his Yorkist predecessors. For others the advent of the Tudors became a cause for regret. Four years after Bosworth, Henry Percy was publicly murdered near

Thirsk while levying a particularly burdensome tax for his new master. The Yorkshiremen thus delivered their own judgement on Percy's betrayal of Richard and on the rapacity of Henry VII. Morbid suspicion was Henry's other vice: in 1492 it claimed the life of Sir William Stanley, who was beheaded on a charge of conspiring with the pretender Perkin Warbeck. Three years later the Milanese ambassador reported that 'the king is rather feared than loved... if fortune allowed some lord of the blood royal to rise and he had to take the field, he would fare badly owing to his avarice; his people would abandon him'.

Dr Thomas Langton, Bishop of St David's and later of Salisbury, recorded another verdict: 'He contents the people where he goes best that ever did prince; for many a poor man that hath suffered wrong many days have been relieved and helped by him.... God hath sent him to us for the weal of us all.' But he was writing about Richard.

Epilogue

Richard Reclaimed

One Saturday afternoon in late August 2012 the driver of a six-ton red digger worked his machine's sharp-edged bucket below the surface of a car park in Leicester and cut through a length of human bone. It was the first day of excavation on a two-week archaeological project, the official aim of which was to look for the ruins of a long-vanished religious house known as the Greyfriars. The digger was working in the first trench to be opened up.

The discovery of human remains on the presumed site of the Greyfriars was not a surprise. The buildings that once stood there included a church, and medieval churches were places where people were buried. But the appearance of a thighbone meant two complications arose.

In the first place, there was now paperwork to complete: in the UK, the Ministry of Justice strictly controls permission and protocol for excavating human remains. In the second place there was excitement to contain.

Although the academics involved in the Greyfriars dig had been careful to frame the project as an investigation into the remains of that institution, their work had long been billed to the media as something else. This was, in the public imagination, a dig to look for the lost bones of King Richard III.

The driving personality behind this quest – a quixotic mission, considered by most experts to have vanishingly little chance of success – was an advertising executive-turned-amateur screenwriter named Philippa Langley. For nearly fifteen years, Langley had been interested in Richard. In 2004 she was working on a script about his life when she visited Leicester, walked across the council car park and felt a strange chill, which she interpreted as a sign that she had passed over the dead king's grave.

Following that experience Langley began to consider how to organise a dig covering the site where she believed Richard was buried. In 2011 she contacted Richard Buckley, co-director of the University of Leicester's Archaeological Services and proposed an excavation on the site. Having interested Buckley, she encouraged other parties to join them, including the Richard III Society and Leicester City Council. A television production company, Darlow Smithson Productions, was engaged with a small amount of funding from the UK broadcaster Channel 4.

The result was that, when the dig began in August 2012, it had captured the attention of newspaper and television reporters as well as historians. In one sense, a human skeleton uncovered amid the outline of a friary church was, on its own, nothing more than that. But given the expectation that had been cultivated around the dig – which included bringing fifteenth-century re-enactors on site for a press photo-call – it was enough to drive speculation that the king of England killed at Bosworth 527 years earlier might finally have been tracked down.

* * *

What happened to Richard III after the Battle of Bosworth was for centuries a matter of some confusion. The chroniclers thought they knew. The Croyland Abbey annalist recorded that Richard fell in battle, bravely, as a great prince ought to do; that his body was abused before being taken to Leicester for public display. John Rous and Polydore Vergil, writing later, agreed that Richard was buried in the church of the Greyfriars, without ceremony befitting his royal rank.

In the 1490s, Henry VII commissioned a tomb for his vanquished rival, which was topped with an alabaster effigy. However, after the dissolution of the monasteries, which took place in the late 1530s, the church was destroyed and the tomb was dismantled; by the early seventeenth century the effigy had been replaced by a stone pillar in the garden of a well-to-do citizen named Robert Herrick. In 1612 Herrick showed the pillar to Christopher Wren senior (father of the architect who later designed St Paul's, as well as the urn in which the presumed remains of the Princes in the Tower are today stored). He recorded having admired it in a letter.

By and by, however, this monument also disappeared, and what was at one time a well-marked spot became a vague local memory, and then not even that. A tale arose that when the monasteries were being dissolved, a mob had opened Richard's tomb and removed his bones, parading them through the city before hurling them into the River Soar. The antiquary John Speede alleged that the stone coffin in which the king's corpse had lain was 'made a drinking trough for horses at a common inn, and retaineth the only memory of this monarch's greatness'.

That legend found its way into enough history books to come to be regarded as hard fact. It was even recorded on the official website of the British Monarchy. But there were those – including Langley – who were doubtful. Langley and others believed that Richard remained buried in the Greyfriars. And they thought the truth – or otherwise – of the rumour could be tested if the church of the Greyfriars were to be excavated, and any human remains within it examined.

For many of those people involved in the Leicester dig of 2012, this was the ultimate aim of the project. For others, however, it was a futile ambition, out of step with archaeological good practice.

Once the remains given the official designation Skeleton 1 were lifted from the ground, on 4 and 5

September 2012, these arguments moved from the realm of theoretical to the practical. Here was a skeleton, found where Richard was thought to have been buried.

If these bones were his mortal remains, then scientific analysis ought to be able to say so.

* * *

At first glance, Greyfriars Skeleton 1 was a fair match for Richard. It bore battle wounds. The spine was obviously curved: it belonged to a man who suffered scoliosis, which accorded with the popular image of Richard as a hunchback. It was buried in what appeared to be the choir of the Greyfriars' church, which was exactly where – if the River Soar rumour was false – one would have expected to find it.

Yet there was much more work to be done before any certain verdict could be handed down. The dig in the Leicester car park finished in mid-September 2012. Only on 4 February 2013 was a press conference held by staff from the University of Leicester, led by Richard Buckley, who announced the results of their research, summing them up with the word 'astonishing'.

The initial findings were, briefly put, as follows. Skeleton 1 was male. It was more or less intact, though it was missing its feet, which had been lost when the grave was disturbed during historical building works. The skeleton had a severe curvature in its spine. It had been buried in a rush, perhaps with hands tied, in a sloppily dug grave a little too small for it.

Death had unquestionably been violent. High resolution scans of the bones revealed eleven separate weapon injuries, including dagger wounds to the face and ribcage, sword and halberd wounds to the skull and a further dagger blow probably delivered to the buttocks during post-death mutilation.

Radiocarbon dating suggested with 96 per cent probability that the bones belonged to a man who lived between 1430 and 1530. Tooth samples tested for oxygen and strontium isotopes suggested that this person had grown up in eastern England as a toddler, and thereafter in the west. (Richard was born in Fotheringhay and moved to Ludlow in his youth.) He ate a healthy, upper-class diet rich in protein derived from fish, poultry and pork – though his gut was full of roundworm, a parasite spread by unsanitary living and cooking conditions.

All of these findings were circumstantially consistent with known descriptions of Richard's life and death. But modern science offered further tools of discovery: DNA testing. If a living relative of Richard's could be found, traced back in an unbroken line to a sibling from the House of York, their DNA could be compared to a sample extracted from the skeleton.

There were two stages to this work: a genealogical hunt for someone with provable descent from the Yorkist line; and DNA sequencing of the bones of Skeleton 1. Research by the historians John Ashdown-Hill and Kevin Schürer tracked down two candidates in the first category. They were a London-based Canadian cabinet-maker named Michael Ibsen and an Australian-born researcher called Wendy Duldig.

The DNA analysis to compare samples taken from Ibsen and Duldig with samples taken from Skeleton 1's teeth and thighbone was carried out by Turi King, a geneticist at the University of Leicester. Her findings showed near perfect matches. It was overwhelmingly likely that the bones were indeed Richard III's.

Taken together, Richard Buckley announced to the world's media in February 2013, all this meant there could be very little scientific or historical doubt that Skeleton 1 was Richard. A subsequent study of all the data collected from the Greyfriars placed the likelihood at somewhere around 99.999 per cent.

Richard had been found.

* * *

During the eighteenth and nineteenth centuries there was a vogue for opening royal tombs and looking at the bones of kings. In 1774 Edward I's black marble sarcophagus was opened and the king was found well preserved, wrapped in linen, wearing red-and-gold robes. In 1834 Henry IV's body was examined within his tomb at Canterbury Cathedral. In 1871 Plantagenet burial monuments in

Westminster were cleaned and their occupants examined, including the bodies of Henry III and Richard II.

Studies were made of all these royal corpses – sometimes to the detriment of the remains, which in Henry IV's case crumbled into dust on exposure to the outside air. But no British monarch was ever subjected to such close scientific scrutiny as Richard III after his removal from his resting-place beneath a Leicester car park.

Besides the evidence that formally identified Skeleton 1 as Richard, other intriguing, personalising details about the king's life were revealed. DNA analysis revealed that in life Richard very likely had blue eyes, and as a child probably had blond hair. Osteology established that he would have stood at 5'8" tall, though he may have shrunk in adulthood due to his scoliosis, which would probably have lifted his right shoulder higher than his left. Facial modelling based on Richard's skull, carried out at the University of Dundee, produced a lifelike bust of the king, which bore a striking resemblance to the famous portrait displayed in London's National Portrait Gallery. (NPG 148)

A second dig in Leicester in the summer of 2013 brought to light more information about the Greyfriars precinct and church: a medieval floor tile gave a hint as to the decoration of the church at the time that Richard was buried; other high-status graves were discovered, some of which were excavated. Fragments were uncovered of the paths that were once laid in Robert Herrick's garden, along which Christopher Wren Sr once walked as he looked at the marker that identified Richard's burial site, shortly before it disappeared into half a century's oblivion.

Yet, by the time that this second phase of archaeological study was underway, a new focus was emerging for those with an interest in Richard's remains. When previous British monarchs had been exhumed and studied, they had been replaced afterwards in their graves. For Richard this was obviously not possible. So a question arose: where should Richard's remains be reinterred? And how?

In 2012–13, when Richard's remains were being recovered and studied, the question of what to do with them afterwards seemed to be straightforward. The Ministry of Justice licence to exhume stated that Skeleton 1 was to be stored in a museum or buried in Leicester's cathedral.

Yet, once the identification had become a world news event, persons claiming kinship with Richard began to advocate for the right to decide on the matter of his futher repose. Arguments were presented for Richard's reburial at various locations connected to the House of York: Westminster Abbey, Fotheringhay or York Minster. A group calling themselves The Plantagenet Alliance raised a legal case attempting to challenge the terms of the exhumation licence; their case was heard in the High Court in the spring of 2014.

The High Court's judgement fell in favour of the Ministry of Justice, meaning that Richard's remains could be buried in Leicester cathedral as originally envisaged. However, the very fact that the court was required to hear the case was a sign of strange passions that Richard was proving able to stir in people, half a millennium after his death.

* * *

On Sunday 22 March 2015 Richard's bones, which had been stored in Leicester University for two and a half years, were placed into a lead casket, which was in turn sealed inside an oak coffin made by Michael Ibsen and taken to the site of the Battle of Bosworth. From there they were paraded ceremonially to Leicester, thereby retracing approximately a route Richard last took in 1485 when he was freshly dead and slung over the back of a horse.

The following day a Catholic requiem mass was celebrated for Richard's soul in Holy Cross Priory Church, reflecting the fact that he died obedient to Rome. Then, three days later, on Thursday 26 March, a reburial ceremony of novel devising was held in the Anglican cathedral. This service was conducted by the Archbishop of Canterbury, Justin Welby, and a reading was given by the actor Benedict Cumberbatch. Attendees included several members of the royal family. The service was broadcast live on Channel 4, for whom the documentary broadcast about the original dig had been a smash hit.

To prepare for this occasion, Leicester's cathedral had been extensively remodelled, to a budget of £2.5m, raised by public appeal. (Nearby, a £4.5m visitor centre had also been built, introducing tourists to Richard's life story.) Richard was laid in a new tomb, made from Swaledale limestone mined in Yorkshire and polished until it gleamed.

The reburial ceremony – not quite a funeral, although it was approached that way by some who attended – was meant to lay to rest at last the bones of the maligned last Plantagenet king. Once the tomb was sealed, the bones – including even the tiniest samples extracted for study – were to be left permanently to rest.

Yet, while it brought to a close the phase of research and investigation that began in 2012, Richard's reburial also began a new cycle of speculation concerning other aspects of his life and reign.

Having successfully divined the location of Richard's remains, Langley established a new project to locate the lost ruins of Reading Abbey in Berkshire, where the Norman king Henry I (r. 1100–35) was buried. (At the time of writing this project had not broken ground.) Meanwhile, she maintained an interest in historical questions relating to Richard.

In 2015 she launched the Missing Princes Project: a 'Cold Case History investigation employing the same principles and practices as a modern police investigation', with the aim of turning up new evidence in the case of the

Princes in the Tower. In 2023 this project announced the end of 'Phase One' of its research, when Langley released a book and television programme proposing the thesis that the Princes in the Tower survived Richard's reign.

Her claim was, in essence, that two young men called Lambert Simnel and Perkin Warbeck, best known as the 'pretenders' to Henry VII's throne, were in fact the Princes in the Tower. This claim rested on the evidence of a number of documents uncovered in European archives, including a receipt for weapons supposedly supplied to a son of Edward IV, and the draft of a letter from the Holy Roman Emperor Maximilian I to Henry VII, attempting to persuade him that the pretender Perkin Warbeck was indeed the younger of the Princes, based on certain physical characteristics.

These documents were presented as conclusive evidence that the Princes had survived, and that by extension Richard III was innocent of regicide. As a number of historians pointed out in response, this evidence was in fact far from secure. The case of the Princes in the Tower remains one of the most emotionally charged mysteries in English medieval history. If it is ever to be satisfactorily advanced, let alone solved, the answer most likely lies in forensic analysis of the skeletons discovered beneath a staircase in the White Tower in 1674.

Be that as it may, the story of Richard, the 'king in the car park', succeeded completely in capturing public imagination in the decade following the Leicester dig.

A feature film entitled *The Lost King* was released in 2022, breezily warping the story of the dig into a great British underdog narrative. Real individuals depicted in the film protested on its release that their roles had been distorted in the telling. But if this meant that the film bore a similarly loose relation to documented history as other great dramas penned about Richard III's life and reign, it was perhaps entirely fitting.

Dan Jones
Staines-upon-Thames
February 2025

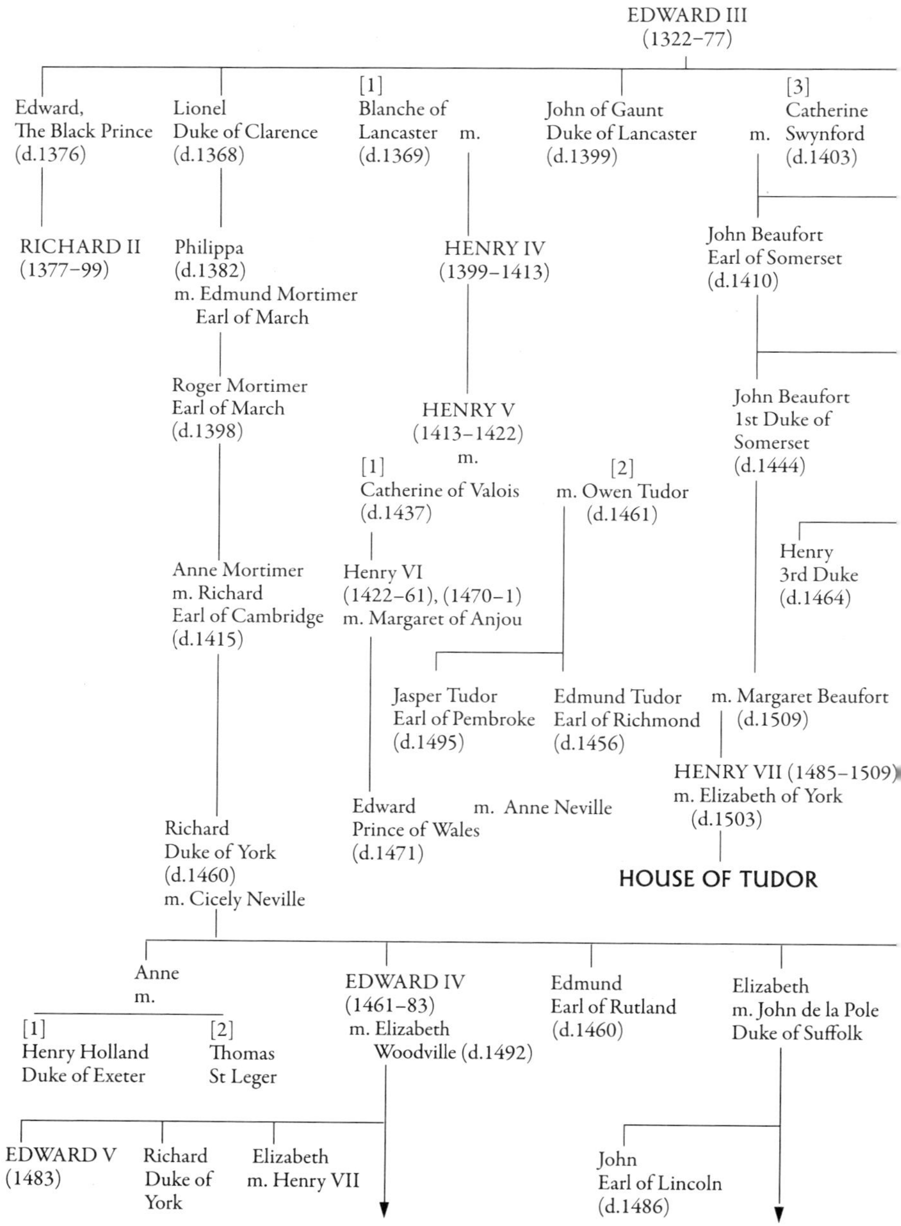
EDWARD III
(1322–77)
Edward,
The Black Prince
(d.1376)
Lionel
Duke of Clarence
(d.1368)
[1]
Blanche of
Lancaster
(d.1369)
m.
John of Gaunt
Duke of Lancaster
(d.1399)
m.
[3]
Catherine
Swynford
(d.1403)
RICHARD II
(1377–99)
Philippa
(d.1382)
m. Edmund Mortimer
Earl of March
HENRY IV
(1399–1413)
John Beaufort
Earl of Somerset
(d.1410)
Roger Mortimer
Earl of March
(d.1398)
HENRY V
(1413–1422)
m.
John Beaufort
1st Duke of
Somerset
(d.1444)
[1]
Catherine of Valois
(d.1437)
[2]
m. Owen Tudor
(d.1461)
Henry
3rd Duke
(d.1464)
Anne Mortimer
m. Richard
Earl of Cambridge
(d.1415)
Henry VI
(1422–61), (1470–1)
m. Margaret of Anjou
Jasper Tudor
Earl of Pembroke
(d.1495)
Edmund Tudor
Earl of Richmond
(d.1456)
m. Margaret Beaufort
(d.1509)
HENRY VII (1485–1509)
m. Elizabeth of York
(d.1503)
Edward
Prince of Wales
(d.1471)
m. Anne Neville
Richard
Duke of York
(d.1460)
m. Cicely Neville
HOUSE OF TUDOR
Anne
m.
[1]
Henry Holland
Duke of Exeter
[2]
Thomas
St Leger
EDWARD IV
(1461–83)
m. Elizabeth
Woodville (d.1492)
Edmund
Earl of Rutland
(d.1460)
Elizabeth
m. John de la Pole
Duke of Suffolk
EDWARD V
(1483)
Richard
Duke of
York
Elizabeth
m. Henry VII
John
Earl of Lincoln
(d.1486)

Edmund Langley
Duke of York
(d.1402)

Thomas of
Woodstock
Duke of Gloucester
(d.1397)

Henry,
Cardinal Beaufort
(d.1447)

Joan Beaufort
m. Ralph Neville
Earl of Westmorland
(d.1425)

Richard
Earl of Cambridge
(d.1415)
m. Anne Mortimer

Anne
m. Edmund
Earl of Stafford
(d.1403)

Edmund Beaufort
2nd Duke of
Somerset
(d.1455)

Richard Neville
Earl of Salisbury
(d.1460)

Cecily
Neville
m.
Richard
Duke of York
(d.1460)

Humphrey
Earl of Stafford
1st Duke of
Buckingham
(d.1460)

HOUSE OF YORK

Edmund
4th Duke
(d.1471)

John
(d.1471)

Richard Neville
Earl of Warwick
(The Kingmaker)
(d.1470)
m. Anne Beauchamp

Humphrey
(d.1455)

Henry Stafford
2nd Duke of
Buckingham
(d.1483)

Isabel
m. George
Duke of Clarence

Anne
m.

[1]
Edward
Prince of Wales

[2]
Richard
Duke of Gloucester

Margaret
m. Charles
Duke of Burgundy
(d.1477)

George
Duke of Clarence
(d.1478)
m. Isabel Neville
(d.1476)

RICHARD III
(1483–5)
m. Anne Neville
(d.1485)

Edward
Earl of Warwick
(d.1499)

Margaret Pole
Countess of Salisbury
(d.1541)

Edward
Prince of Wales
(d.1484)

Select Bibliography

For the study of Richard and his contemporaries there is no more readable or scholarly guide than Paul Murray Kendall, whose four books are listed below with others of relevant interest.

H. S. Bennett, *The Pastons and their England* (1922)

Michael Bennett, *The Battle of Bosworth* (1985)

George Buck, *History of King Richard III, 1619*, ed. A. N. Kincaid (1979)

S. B. Chrimes, *Henry VII* (1972)

David R. Cook, *Lancastrians and Yorkists: The Wars of the Roses* (1984)

William Cornwallis, *Encomium of Richard III*, ed. A. N. Kincaid (1977)

James Gairdner, *History of the Life and Reign of Richard III* (rev. ed., 1898)

Anthony Goodman, *The Wars of the Roses: Military Activity and English Society 1452–1497* (1981)

P. W. Hammond, *Richard III: The Road to Bosworth Field* (1985)

Alison Hanham, *Richard III and His Early Historians 1483–1535* (1975)

E. F. Jacob, *The Fifteenth Century 1399–1485* (2nd ed., 1961)
R. H. Jarman, *We Speak No Treason* (1971)
Paul Murray Kendall, *Richard III* (1955)
*Warwick the Kingmake*r (1957)
The Yorkist Age (1962)
Louis XI (1971)
C. L. Kingsford, *Prejudice and Promise in Fifteenth-Century England* (1925)
V. B. Lamb, *The Betrayal of Richard III* (1959)
J. R. Lander, *The Wars of the Roses* (1965)
Philip Lindsay, *King Richard III* (1933)
David MacGibbon, Elizabeth Woodville (1938)
Dominic Mancini, *The Usurpation of Richard III*, ed. C. A. J. Armstrong (2nd ed., 1969)
Sir Clements Markham, *Richard III: His Life and Character* (1906)
R. J. Mitchell, *John Tiptoft* (1938)
Thomas More, *The History of King Richard III*, ed. R. S. Sylvester (the Yale edition of the Complete Works of St Thomas More, vol. 2, 1963)
Richard Marius, *Thomas More* (1984)
Alec R. Myers, *England in the Late Middle Ages* (1952)
'The Character of Richard III' in *History Today*, vol. 4 (1954)
Alec R. Myers, *The Household of Edward IV* (1959)
A. J. Pollard, *The Wars of the Roses* (1988)
Jeremy Potter, *Good King Richard? An Account of Richard III and His Reputation 1483–1983* (1983)
Sir James Ramsay, *Lancaster and York* (2 vols, 1892)

Charles Ross, *The Wars of the Roses: A Concise History* (1976)
Richard III (1981)
A. L. Rowse, *Bosworth Field and the Wars of the Roses* (1966)
Giles St Aubyn, *The Year of Three Kings 1483* (1983)
Cora L. Scofield, *The Life and Reign of Edward IV* (2 vols, 1923)
Desmond Seward, *Richard III: England's Black Legend* (1983)
Horace Walpole, *Historic Doubts on the Life and Reign of King Richard III* (1768; reprinted 1974)

Image Credits

In-text Images

p.16 Royal Collection Trust © His Majesty King Charles III 2022
p.20 From the British Library archive / Bridgeman Images
p.21 From the British Library archive / Bridgeman Images
pp.32-3 incamerastock / Alamy
p.40 Smith Archive / Alamy
p.46 Photo 12 / Alamy
p.50 claudiodivizia / Getty Images
p.51 Granger – Historical Picture Archive / Alamy
p.67 Provided by Ghent University Library
p.86 Allan Baxter / Getty Images
p.90 World History Archive / Alamy
p.100 By permission of The Dean and Canons of Windsor
p.101 By permission of The Dean and Canons of Windsor
p.102 sparkypus.com
p.115 Smith Archive / Alamy
p.125 The Reading Room / Alamy
p.135 Hoberman Publishing / Alamy
p.142 (left) World History Archive / Alamy
p.142 (right) Photo 12 / Alamy
p.143 ART Collection / Alamy
p.153 The Tallow Chandlers' Company

p.171 Bashford Dean Memorial Collection / The Metropolitan Museum of Art
p.180 Charles O. Cecil / Alamy
p.190 Smith Archive / Alamy
p.191 Photo 12 / Alamy
p.199 Terence Kerr / Alamy
p.213 Loop Images / Contributor / Getty Images

Plate Section Images

1. Genealogy Roll – From the British Library archive / Bridgeman Images
2. The Battle of Barnet – DEA Picture Library / Contributor
3. Edward IV © Canterbury Cathedral / Reproduced courtesy of the Chapter, Canterbury Cathedral / Bridgeman Images
4. Anthony Woodville Presenting the *Dictes* – The Picture Art Collection / Alamy
5. Canterbury Cathedral Stained Glass © Canterbury Cathedral / Reproduced courtesy of the Chapter, Canterbury Cathedral / Bridgeman Images
6. Rous Roll – From the British Library archive / Bridgeman Images
7. Anne Neville – The History Collection / Alamy
8. Richard III – Bridgeman Images
9. John Howard – Lisby / Wikimedia Commons / CC BY SA 4.0
10. Elizabeth of York – The Picture Art Collection / Alamy
11. Sheriff Hutton Castle – Print Collector / Contributor / Getty Images
12. Richard III – Art Collection 3 / Alamy
13. Henry Tudor – Prism Archivo / Alamy
14. Princes in the Tower – Bridgeman Images

Index

Illustrations and captions are indicated by numbers in *italics*.

V

W